REVOLUTION

Volume 20

THE PEOPLE'S REPUBLICS OF EASTERN EUROPE

THE PEOPLE'S REPUBLICS OF EASTERN EUROPE

JÜRGEN TAMPKE

LONDON AND NEW YORK

First published in 1983 by Croom Helm Ltd

This edition first published in 2022
by Routledge
4 Park Square, Milton Park, Abingdon, Oxon OX14 4RN

and by Routledge
605 Third Avenue, New York, NY 10158

Routledge is an imprint of the Taylor & Francis Group, an informa business

© 1983 Jürgen Tampke

All rights reserved. No part of this book may be reprinted or reproduced or utilised in any form or by any electronic, mechanical, or other means, now known or hereafter invented, including photocopying and recording, or in any information storage or retrieval system, without permission in writing from the publishers.

Trademark notice: Product or corporate names may be trademarks or registered trademarks, and are used only for identification and explanation without intent to infringe.

British Library Cataloguing in Publication Data
A catalogue record for this book is available from the British Library

ISBN: 978-1-032-12623-4 (Set)
ISBN: 978-1-003-26095-0 (Set) (ebk)
ISBN: 978-1-032-17068-8 (Volume 20) (hbk)
ISBN: 978-1-032-17074-9 (Volume 20) (pbk)
ISBN: 978-1-003-25168-2 (Volume 20) (ebk)

DOI: 10.4324/9781003251682

Publisher's Note
The publisher has gone to great lengths to ensure the quality of this reprint but points out that some imperfections in the original copies may be apparent.

Disclaimer
The publisher has made every effort to trace copyright holders and would welcome correspondence from those they have been unable to trace.

The People's Republics of Eastern Europe

JÜRGEN TAMPKE

CROOM HELM
London & Canberra

©1983 Jürgen Tampke
Croom Helm Ltd, Provident House, Burrell Row,
Beckenham, Kent BR3 1AT

British Library Cataloguing in Publication Data

Tampke, Jürgen
　　The people's republics of Eastern Europe
　　1. Europe, Eastern – History – 20th Century
　　I. Title
　　947　　DJK50
　　ISBN 0-7099-2415-1

Printed and bound in Great Britain by
Biddles Ltd, Guildford and King's Lynn

CONTENTS

Introduction

1	The Emergence of the New Eastern Europe (1943-7)	9
2	Planned Economy and Cold War (1948-53)	31
3	Confrontation and Consolidation (1954-9)	43
4	The Hungarian People's Republic: Liberal Socialism?	54
5	The German Democratic Republic: Economic Miracle?	68
6	Romania: Mediator between East and West?	83
7	Czechoslovakia 1968: A Reappraisal	93
8	The Polish People's Republic: Catholics and Cultivators	114
9	Yugoslavia: Communist League and Workers' Councils	126
10	Towards a Consumer Society	139
11	Convergence or Divergence	154
12	Recreation and Entertainment	163
Index		173

INTRODUCTION

For more than a decade relations between the countries of Eastern and Western Europe have been steadily improving. A long-term tendency towards *rapprochement*, which pre-dates the Ostpolitik of the Brandt Government in the late 1960s, continued throughout the 1970s to a climax with the signing of the 1976 Helsinki accords, when 35 European states, the USA and Canada signed a long-term programme for the realisation of peaceful coexistence. The policy of detente is not supported by all political opinions and there have been serious setbacks such as the decision of the NATO countries to establish medium-range nuclear missiles in Western Europe and the recent controversy over the events in Poland, the Moscow Olympics and the Afghanistan issue. It is, however, likely that the spirit of Helsinki will persist. More than a decade of sustained cultural exchanges, sporting contacts, tourism and especially growing trade between the nations of Eastern and Western Europe preclude a return to ideological confrontation as in the Cold War years. Most government and public opinion favours the political *status quo* in Europe, no doubt realising that the price of drastic change would be too high.

Although a trend away from the simplistic 'black and white' presentations of the Cold War era has been evident for some time, publications on this topic continue to be written almost exclusively from a Western point of view and therefore lack understanding of the Eastern European perspective.[1] By incorporating historical evidence from both East and West, and by avoiding both *denunciamentos* and apologies, it is intended that this work will make a contribution to our understanding of the contemporary situation.

The first chapter deals with the establishment of the People's Republics after the Second World War. It questions the view commonly presented that the Soviet Union as it advanced into Eastern Europe imposed a ring of satellites under puppet communist regimes upon a reluctant population.[2]

Chapters two and three discuss the economic and political difficulties of the early fifties, the ensuing confrontations of the mid-1950s and their eventual settlement. The subsequent three chapters deal with the achievements and dynamics of Eastern European Socialism. The history of the Hungarian People's Republic under Janos Kadar's government with its trend towards liberal socialism, the economic performance of the GDR and Romania's foreign policies are examined.

This is followed by three chapters which analyse some of the problems of Eastern European Socialism: the policies of the Czechoslovakian Communist movement and the 1968 crisis, Poland's economic problems and the issues of the Yugoslav Council system.

The remainder of the book covers the People's Republics throughout the seventies and concludes with some observations on life in Eastern Europe and on the outlook for the future.

Notes

1. J.F. Brown, *The New Eastern Europe, The Khrushchev Era and After* (Pall Mall Press, London, 1966); P. Calvocoressi, *World Politics Since 1945* (Longman, London, 1977); M. McCauley, *Communist Power in Europe 1944-49* (Macmillan, London, 1977); A. Polonski, *The Little Dictators, The History of Eastern Europe since 1918* (Routledge and Kegan Paul, London, 1975); F.R. Willis, *Europe in the Global Age* (New York, 1975); S. Fischer-Galati, *The Communist Parties of Eastern Europe* (Columbia Press, New York, 1979).

2. For the classical account see H. Seton-Watson, *The East European Revolution* (Methuen, London, 1956).

Acknowledgements

This project was made possible through the financial assistance of the University of New South Wales and the hospitality of the Humboldt Universtät which gave me access to a wide range of sources. I would also like to thank my friends in Eastern and Western Europe and in Australia with whom I discussed the issues raised by this study. However, I must stress that I bear the sole responsibility for the views and arguments presented in this book. I owe special thanks to Günter Rose, Eveline, John Perkins and most of all to Colin Doxford for his generous help.

Jürgen Tampke

1 THE EMERGENCE OF THE NEW EASTERN EUROPE (1943-7)

European history since the middle of the nineteenth century has been characterised by social confrontation. The antagonists have been broadly labelled as the 'establishment', which originally comprised the traditional elite centred upon crown, Church and aristocracy, and the left. As the nineteenth century and modern industrialisation progressed this elite absorbed the entrepreneurial and professional middle classes. Subsequently, at least in Western Europe these traditional forces, which were not necessarily opposed to progress *qua* progress, proved themselves capable of absorbing the moderate workers' movement that broadly accepted the *status quo* in respect of the structure of class society and hoped to introduce gradual social and economic reform. The opponents of this historical consensus, left-wing socialists, anarchists and especially revolutionary Marxists were bent upon the overthrow of the established order and its replacement by a socially and economically egalitarian society. They had their supporters: initially they were drawn from the dissatisfied and impoverished artisan class, but with the spread of industrialisation the protest came to include broader sections of the working class. In some parts of Europe, more particularly in South and South-eastern Europe, radical left-wing thought also permeated the rural areas.

Until the First World War the political establishment overcame all these challenges with little difficulty. The Paris Commune and the Russian Revolution of 1905, for example, were soon suppressed, although they hinted at the growing support the opposition to the system was gaining. At the end of the First World War the revolutionary potential which had accumulated in Europe became fully evident for the first time. In fact many historians today maintain that the war itself was the subsummation and the product of Europe's domestic crisis rather than the result of a breakdown of international diplomacy.[1] They argue that the economic and social tension brought about by industrialisation had engendered such a serious crisis in society that governments embarked upon adventurous and essentially aggressive foreign policies to divert attention from the domestic contradictions and to rally the people in support of the *status quo*. For the Hapsburg, Hohenzollern and Romanov dynasties, the war for their survival ironically led to their undoing and a wave of revolution spread throughout Central and Eastern Europe between 1917 and 1920.

Following the Soviet model that emerged in Russia, workers' councils were set up in a number of centres. With the one decisive Russian exception, this first major confrontation ended with the defeat of the revolutionary left. Divisions amongst themselves, lack of capable leadership and the residual vitality of liberal ideals in the West of Europe were among the factors which ensured that by 1920 the pre-war consensus was able to re-establish itself. For Eastern Europe, however, the outcome of the First World War only intensified historical conflicts. Governments in Southern and Eastern Europe increasingly moved to the political right, with most states by the 1930s becoming semi-Fascist if not outright Fascist. Nevertheless, the defeat and discredit of Fascism by 1945 in Germany and in Eastern Europe left communism in a strong if not an invincible position.

The situation that enabled the communists to challenge the old order in Eastern Europe[2] arose from four major factors. These were: the political, economic and social record of the inter-war governments, the traumatic experience and national disaster of the Second World War, the general swing in Europe to the left, which was largely brought about by the determined opposition to Fascism of communists and finally — important, but not as central as many historians maintain — the victory of the Soviet troops over Germany.

The countries that were liberated by Soviet troops and which today constitute the people's republics of Eastern Europe emerged from the disintegration of four empires: the Turkish, Russian, Austro-Hungarian and German. Bulgaria, Romania, Albania and the Serbian parts of what was to become Yugoslavia arose in the nineteenth century, as the territory of the 'sick man of Europe' was gradually pushed eastwards. The new Poland was made up of former German, Austrian and Russian territories. The latter also conceded Bessarabia to Romania. The new order in Europe emerged primarily as a result of the collapse of the Austro-Hungarian empire.

The year 1918 saw the collapse of the old Danube monarchy. After nearly half a millenium of existence as a great — at times even the leading — power, in 1918 it finally succumbed to the logic of its internal national contradictions. Ideas of a multinational community of nations did not seem to belong to the twentieth century and the aspirations for national independence. For 50 years nationals and liberals amongst the numerous ethnic groups of the Hapsburg empire had demanded independence; now at last they had succeeded. Hungary, Czechoslovakia and Yugoslavia joined the ranks of small states in that part of Europe. It soon emerged, however, that the new arrangement was even more fragile than the empire it had replaced.

As is well known, the post First World War peace treaties did not solve problems of nationality in Eastern Europe. Czechoslovakia consisted of a majority of Czechs and Slovaks but one-third of its 15 million people comprised national minorities of Poles, Ruthenians, Hungarians and especially Germans. In Poland only two-thirds of its population were Polish and in Yugoslavia, in addition to the conflict between Serbs and Croats, there were 1.7 million Albanians, Hungarians and Germans in a total population of 12 million.

Romania profited considerably from the First World War. It not only annexed Bessarabia in the wake of the Bolshevik Revolution in Russia, but it also incorporated Transylvania and other parts of Eastern Hungary and came to include 1½ million Hungarians among its population.

It was the Romanian expansion that occasioned a prolongation of the war beyond the armistice. When the Hungarian government under Mihaly Karolyi failed to stop the loss of territory, Budapest saw the establishment of a Soviet government under Bela Kun. With widespread support in Budapest, a communist-social democratic government was set up on 20 March 1919 headed by Kun and the leaders of the social democrats, Sigismund Kunfi and Alexander Gabai. Other noticeable ministers in the Hungarian revolutionary government included the Hungarian post Second World War Communist Party leader Matyas Rakosi and the philosopher Georg Lukacz. Edicts ordered the socialisation of housing, banks, retail distribution and the land, and the rigorous suppression of black market activities; even aristocratic sports such as racing were forbidden. The Kun Government repelled the Romanian invasion of Hungary but failed to maintain power in Budapest. The Hungarian proletarian dictatorship was harsh but there was less terror under Kun than under the White regime that followed. The counter-revolution led by Admiral Horthy and supported by Romanian troops was responsible for the deaths of thousands of workers suspected of supporting the Kun Government. Few Communists survived. Those who did went underground for the next 25 years or escaped to the Soviet Union.

One year later Poland and the Soviet Union were also at war. Like the Romanians, the Polish government hoped to benefit from the collapse of Tsarism in Russia. A very generous interpretation of Poland's Eastern boundaries before her partition by Prussia, Russia and Austria in the eighteenth century led the Polish government to claim White Russia,

Lithuania and Ukrainian territories. But by 1920 the Red Army was strong enough to counter the Polish forces; in fact the Soviet troops almost reached Warsaw in their counter-offensive. The Allies were not favourably disposed towards the creation of a Greater Poland and agreed to the 'Curzon line', which is basically the Polish-Soviet frontier today. Nevertheless a final drive by the Polish general Josef Pilsudski managed to establish the inter-war boundary just west of Minsk, far into White Russia.

In the other countries the problem of ethnicity, nationality and territory did not lead to all-out war but the nationality problem lingered. In Yugoslavia the division between Serbs and Croats remained bitter throughout, with the crisis reaching a peak in 1928 when the leader of the Croatian Peasant Party, Stjepan Radic, was assassinated in the Belgrade parliament. Most bellicose on the issue of national minorities was the country which was comparatively least affected by the outcome of the war, namely Germany. Admittedly not every German lived in the territory administered by the Weimar Republic but compared to the Austro-Hungarian empire and also to Russia, the German losses in territory and people imposed by the peace treaty were modest. The most outspoken group of Germans outside the Republic, the Sudeten Germans, had never belonged to the German empire. Nevertheless it is with the Sudeten Germans that the demagogic factors associated with passionate and violent nationalism reveal themselves most clearly in the 1930s. Then the Sudeten Nazi Party, supported by the Hitler Government, used the nationality issue to bring about the destruction of Czechoslovakia.

Serious as the nationality problem was, it was not the main issue in Eastern Europe between the wars. More important was the nature of the political system. Great hopes were held for post-war liberal parliamentary democracy but the spirit of Versailles, with its slogans of democracy and national freedom, did not fall on very fertile soil in the new states. The Hungarian Prime Minister Karolyi, with his idea of a liberal Hungary forming part of a Danubian democratic federation, was the first to be disillusioned when his country's neighbours attacked the remnant of the former Hungarian part of the dual monarchy. After the brief episode of Bela Kun, Hungary was the first country to turn to a thinly veiled dictatorship under Admiral Horthy. Bulgaria too never saw the emergence of genuine democratic government. Between 1919 and 1923 there was the so-called 'dictatorship of the village over the town'. Here the Agrarian Party and its leader, Alexander Stamvalishy, pursued an anti-middle-class, anti-urban policy which was chiefly concerned with the economic well-being of the peasantry. The subsequent ten years saw the country shaken by waves of terrorism from both left and right, which did not abate until a coup in 1934 established a military dictatorship.

The sophisticated democratic system did not work well in Poland either. An impressive legal and parliamentary system was created in March 1921, with a constitution based on the third French Republic. This gave the supreme power to a democratically elected Lower House (the Sejm) leaving a limited power of veto to the Upper House and the President. The radical difference between this and previous forms of government in Poland, together with the introduction of proportional representation and the exuberant individualism of the Polish intelligentsia, soon led to difficulties. With 92 political parties there was extreme atomisation, to say the least. In 1927 Marshall Pilsudski decided to put an end to 'the chaos' and established a military dictatorship.

In Yugoslavia, a year after Radic's assassination in 1928, the King declared a royal dictatorship. Following a decade of genuine attempts to make constitutional government and liberal institutions work, Romania followed suit in 1930 when the King assumed full control of government to establish a ruthless and corrupt regime. Albania's history was marred by the deep division between the Moslem, Catholic and Orthodox faiths and between the still largely tribal peoples of the northern mountains and the developed plainsmen of the south. In December 1924 Ahmed Zogu, a tribal chieftain from the north, seized power. With Italian military and economic support he consolidated his position and had himself declared King of Albania in 1928. Italian influence continued to grow during the 1930s until the country became a formal protectorate of fascist Italy in April 1939.

By 1938, therefore, with the exception of Czechoslovakia, where democratic institutions survived until the German dismemberment of the nation, parliamentary government had failed to survive in Eastern Europe. There was considerable disillusionment with party politics among most sections of the population. The British historian, James Joll, sums up the inter-war history of Eastern Europe aptly when he concludes that 'peopled by a backward and impoverished peasantry and lacking administrative experience − these countries did not have the substructure of the political traditions to sustain a sophisticated party system of government'.[3]

The unimpressive political record of the nations of Eastern Europe during the inter-war years is not only to be explained by the lack of a parliamentary or liberal tradition. An even more important reason lies in the economic weakness which was characteristic of all these countries including Czechoslovakia. The Austro-Hungarian empire had formed an economic entity which before the First World War had all economic sectors showing annual rates of increased production of the order of 3 to 4 per cent. The economic fragmentation caused by the outcome of the First World War brought the growth rate down to 1.5 per cent in all countries with the exception of Bulgaria.[4]

Modernisation, which began in the late nineteenth century, was halted and failed to achieve the earlier anticipated stage of development. In fact, some sectors of the economy evinced complete stagnation. In others, growth was modest and proceeded without producing general socio-economic advancement. The development of railways, which constituted the backbone of the pre-First World War industrial dynamism of the region, came to a halt. This of course was also the case in the advanced industrial countries of Western Europe. However, not only was the railway density in Eastern and South-eastern Europe far below that of the Western countries when stagnation set in but, in addition, the shift towards more modern means of transport (road and air) which accompanied railway stagnation in the West, failed to occur. The retarded development of motor transport is illustrated by the motorisation indicator which gives the number of motor vehicles in relation to the area and population of the country. By 1938 this stood at an average of 5.7 in Western European countries compared to 1.8 in Czechoslovakia, 0.5 in Hungary and 0.3 in Poland, Yugoslavia and Romania.[5] Nor did the continued development of heavy industry which took place in Western Europe up to the outbreak of the Second World War (fostered by the growth of consumer goods) occur in Eastern Europe. It is clear that before the Second World War development in heavy industry was the decisive indicator of the level of industrial development. Consequently, the lack of development of heavy industry, and especially the underdeveloped state of machine industry, was a vital factor explaining the poor industrial performance of the Eastern and South-eastern countries.

The agricultural sector also performed poorly. Land reforms which (except in Hungary and Poland) occurred shortly after the war made distribution of land more equitable. But there were few signs of genuine progress in production as inter-war European agriculture struggled 'against the Scylla of unprofitable tiny plots and the Charibdys of big estates swallowing up everything'.[6] There were few advances in agricultural mechanisation and the use of artificial fertilisers remained at a low

The Emergence of the New Eastern Europe (1943-7)

level. Slow industrial growth meant that cities and towns were unable to absorb the growing surplus of rural labour occasioned by a rapid growth of population, so that the rural sector witnessed growing underemployment.

Not surprisingly, the national income in Eastern Europe was well below the European average. With an average annual national income in Europe of US$200 in 1937, Czechoslovakia reached $170, Hungary $120, Poland $100, Romania $81, Yugoslavia $80 and Bulgaria $75. By contrast, Great Britain, the leader in Europe at the time, reached $440, Sweden $400 and even Nazi Germany, not known for its affluence, had an average national income per capita of $340. Thus the slow and inept modernisation of economic life failed to produce necessary changes in the economy of Eastern Europe but instead increased the contradictions of the pre-First World War years: contradictions which were manifested by the contrast between rural districts and towns, between agriculture and the more modern branches of economy. Cartellisation and foreign ownership continued, further illustrating the fact that there was no change in the fundamental structure of the economy. Whereas in the early years of the century economic growth was associated with rising living standards, the inter-war years did not bring any increase in the real income of the population. As the Hungarian economic historians, Ivan Berend and Gyoergy Ranki sum it up, 'Eastern and South-Eastern Europe became an area struggling with permanent crisis and fraught with inner contradictions in a tense explosive atmosphere where everything called for change'.[7]

The process towards a radical political solution in Eastern Europe was accelerated by the Second World War. Although all countries of Eastern Europe suffered large-scale destruction, the impact of the war varied considerably from country to country. Hungary, Bulgaria and Romania, who fought on Germany's side and who virtually became satellites of the Reich, at least escaped German occupation. As part of the German *Grossraum* economy, they were economically exploited and many of their men died fighting in support of German expansionism. However, with the exception of their Jewish populations, these countries escaped the brutal subjugation that occurred wherever the Germans were directly in control. Large-scale destruction did not reach them until the final stages of war, when they were caught in the struggle between the Red Army and the retreating fascist forces.

Czechoslovakia, although a German-occupied country, was comparatively fortunate in escaping the worst consequences of German rule. The Slovaks remained relatively unmolested in the semi-autonomous

'Slovakian Republic' although the Czech parts of the former nation became the Protectorates of Bohemia and Moravia and were placed under German military and civilian administration. German economic exploitation of the protectorate was total, as the Czech people were fully integrated into the Nazi war machine. The Czech people suffered from the humiliation of having their nation dismembered and they were ranked as inferior citizens in the German Reich. Some acts of Gestapo violence did take place, most notably the murder of the entire male population of the Lidice village in retaliation for the assassination of Reinhard Heydrich on 27 May 1942. However, with the exception of the Jews, the death toll was far lower than in Yugoslavia, Poland and the Soviet Union, countries that participated in armed resistance to the Reich.

In Yugoslavia it is estimated that one and three-quarter million people — 11 per cent of the population — lost their lives as a result of the war, more than half of the total slaughtered in the newly formed 'Independent State of Croatia', where, for three and a half years the fascist government of Ante Pavelic and his *Ustasa* was so brutal that even the Germans toyed with the idea of replacing it with a more restrained administration. The remainder of the former kingdom of Yugoslavia was placed under German, Italian, Hungarian and Romanian administrations. Throughout the war the fascists were challenged by a most effective partisan resistance movement which, aided by the rugged terrain, pinned down a considerable number of German troops.

In the Soviet Union and Poland, German atrocities reached their peak. Here the German *Lebensraum* philosophy was to have its logical conclusion leaving no space for Slavonic *Untermenschen* ('sub-humans') who at best could look forward to a slave-like existence. Here no mercy was shown. In Poland six million people perished as a result of the war, or one-fifth of the population. The concentration camps that had the highest death tolls were all in Poland — Treblinka, Majdanek, Belsen, Auschwitz, Sobobor and Stutthof. The slaughter, in which the Wehrmacht participated alongside the SS, continued without pause throughout the German occupation.

Auschwitz has become the symbol of it all. It was the masterpiece of German destruction where all the inadequacies of the previous extermination methods were overcome. All methods used so far for the 'final solution' had had their drawbacks. The SS death squadrons, which killed hundreds of thousands of Jewish people as the Wehrmacht rolled East, could not be used in the rest of Europe. Methods of extermination possible in Poland and the Soviet Union could not be readily applied to the subjugated people in the West. To line up thousands of men, women and children who had to dig their own graves before they were mowed down by the machineguns of drunken SS officers and even more brutalised Lithuanian, Latvian and Ukranian collaborators, might go unnoticed in the vast space of the East – but elsewhere, mass murder would quickly have revealed the enormity of German criminality. Auschwitz also overcame the shortcomings of Treblinka and other extermination camps. The use of Zyclon B was far superior and more reliable than engine exhaust gas which had been used previously. Auschwitz was, in a word, more efficient. In two main halls 2,000 people could be gassed at one time – a vast improvement on Treblinka, where is was a mere 200. The process in Auschwitz proceeded like clockwork. As the victims arrived in cattle wagons from all over Europe, officers would direct women with children and old people straight to the halls. Here they were asked to undress for de-lousing. Sometimes a mother, sensing what was to come, tried vainly to hide her child in the pile of clothes but usually it was not until the doors were locked, when the Zyclon B eliminated the supply of oxygen, that the victims knew what the final German solution to the Jewish problem was. Depending on weather conditions it took 3 to 15 minutes before the process was completed – signalled by the end of the screaming. Their bodies were then dragged out, their hair shorn off, gold was removed from their teeth, and the women had their private parts searched for hidden jewellery before their bodies were burned. Those who were spared this horror survived on average for three months in the work camp. Of the approximately 40 million deaths attributable to the Second World War, almost 35 million died in Eastern and South-eastern Europe. In this part of Europe, German barbarity and destruction had removed the last slight chance for anything but a radical political solution.

The history of the communist parties who were preparing to take power as the Red Army pushed back the Germans was a mixed one and varied from country to country. Following the Russian October Revolution communist parties had emerged in all countries of Eastern Europe at the end of the First World War. Only in Czechoslovakia were they able to operate openly for virtually the whole of the inter-war period. Here they competed with the socialists for the support of the working class. The balance was in favour of the socialists during the 1920s, with the communists winning about 13 per cent at elections. During the 1930s, the majority of working-class support shifted gradually in favour of the communists. Noteworthy is the fact that the communist support was not restricted to urban areas; the highest vote scored by a Communist Party in Eastern and South-eastern Europe during the 1920s was in the overwhelmingly agrarian Ruthenian parts of Czechoslovakia (42 per cent). The communists also received strong support in Bulgaria, where they were to become the second largest political party after the war with over 20 per cent of the vote. After some violent confrontations with the government they were outlawed in 1926. In parts of Yugoslavia, too, there was widespread support for the communists. In the 1920 election, for example, they won 36 per cent of the vote in Montenegro and 33 per cent in Yugoslav Macedonia. Here too the party found itself outlawed for most of the inter-war years. In Poland the communists were only permitted to contest one election and, severely handicapped as they were, in 1928 they received 7.9 per cent of the vote. Here again their strongest support was in the predominantly rural areas of eastern Poland where they polled 37.2 per cent of the vote in the Brest district and 29.5 per cent in Nowogrodek.[8] After the Bela Kun Soviet Republic, the communists were outlawed in Hungary and went underground or into exile until the end of the war. Nor were the communists able to come to the fore in Romania or Albania, although their strength increased during the 1930s. Thus, notwithstanding setbacks and persecutions, the communists could rely on a formidable basis of popular support when the outbreak of war initiated an entirely new situation.

There is a vast amount of literature in the West on the emergence of the Socialist People's Republics during and after the Second World War. Most writers maintain that the communists, under the guidance and in alliance with Soviet troops, imposed a series of puppet governments upon a reluctant population. By this interpretation, liberal and democratic elements were tricked into false alliances, and opposition gradually withered away to be replaced by collaborators before eventually a minority communist dictatorship was established. However, it is difficult to see how these interpretations fit the evidence that is available.

Although there are some common features throughout, the establishment of socialist governments varied greatly from country to country. Nevertheless, some generalisations can be made. First, there were those countries where the communists had maintained a position of sufficient strength by the end of the war that — regardless of the Red Army — they would have achieved power. These are Yugoslavia, Albania and, to a degree, Bulgaria. Second, there were those nations where the communists had a modest power base but managed because of their vigorous anti-fascist policies and because of the changing fortunes of the war to rally the majority of the nation behind their cause — although not before a fierce confrontation with their numerous political opponents. This category includes Poland, Romania and, again with some qualification, Hungary. Finally, there were the two industrialised states, Czechoslovakia and the Soviet-occupied zone of Germany — the later German Democratic Republic — where a quite different course of events took place.

Nowhere in the area covered by this book was the victory of the communist-led anti-fascist liberation movement so resounding as in Yugoslavia. The failure of inter-war Yugoslavian governments to keep the country neutral and independent had led to national dismemberment and, after the Soviet Union and Poland, the country suffered the highest casualty rate in Eastern Europe. Resistance began immediately after the German-Italian occupation of April 1941. Initially there were two Yugoslav resistance movements; the predominantly Serbian *cetnik* groups which were made up of remnants of the Royal Army headed by Colonel Anton Mihailovic, and the communist-led partisan movement under Josip Broz, called Tito. The latter comprised all sections of society and all Yugoslav nationalities. Attempts were made to co-ordinate the efforts of the two resistance groups but, given their different composition and aims, these failed. Tito's forces soon emerged as the most effective organisation, controlling considerable parts of Yugoslavia by 1943.

Under communist leadership 'people's committees' established themselves in liberated regions. The 'Anti-Fascist Council for the Liberation of Yugoslavia' (AVNOJ), which was founded in November 1942, was able to establish a provisional government in Jajce one year later. Its declared goal was the liberation of Yugoslavia and the establishment of a broad democratic government recognising the rights of the many ethnic and religious groups in the country. By May 1944 it was clear to Allied observers that Tito had gained the upper hand. The success of the partisans so impressed the Allies that they began to support his troops, withdrawing aid from Mihailovic, who had in fact begun to collaborate with the fascists. Tito agreed to their request that non-communists be included in the government. He gave three ministries to the royal government in London. In September 1944 the King broadcast an appeal from London to all Yugoslav patriots to rally to Tito. One month later, with the aid of a Soviet advance, the country was finally liberated from Fascism. By this time effective control was in the hands of the communists acting through the provisional government at the national level and the people's committees at the local level. In June 1945 all German-held property, as well as that of collaborators, was expropriated and resulted effectively in 80 per cent of Yugoslavia's industry being nationalised. At the same time foreign capital was placed under state control. There were also far-reaching agrarian reforms a month later which redistributed a million hectares of land to landless peasants or state co-operatives. In November 1945 a People's Front, which under communist leadership included representatives from all parts of the community who had participated in the liberation movement, presented itself to the people. At the election there were no opposition candidates although provision was made for dissent by providing ballot boxes for voters who were opposed to the People's Front. Western observers reported no irregularities in an election which gave the People's Front 90 per cent of the vote. The former kingdom of Yugoslavia now officially became the Federal People's Republic of Yugoslavia with the Constituent Assembly becoming its first parliament.

The course of events in Albania was closely linked to that in Yugoslavia. The country had become an Italian colony before the outbreak of the Second World War when Mussolini's troops drove out King Zog and his government in April 1939. Before the Second World War Albania was probably the most backward state in Europe. The majority of the population still existed in a state of feudal dependency, industry barely accounted for one tenth of the gross national product, there were neither railways nor all-weather roads. This state of backwardness and the collaboration of the country's ruling class — feudal landlords, merchants and substantial peasants — with the fascists accounted for the rapidly-growing support of the communist-led National Liberation Movement which, as in Yugoslavia, incorporated all sections of the population. By the end of 1943 the National Liberation Army had already freed the whole of south and central Albania. Pro-royalist forces attempted to stem the communist tide by founding a 'Mutual Front' (*Balli Kombetar*) but they failed to rally sufficient numbers to halt the advance of the National Liberation Movement.

Throughout 1944 local Liberation Councils were founded and in October of that year a provisional government was formed which comprised all sections of the resistance movement under communist leadership. In August 1945 middle-class elements suspected of co-operation with *Balli Kombetar* or *Legalitat*, another anti-communist opposition group, were expelled from the government and in elections to a national assembly two months later the candidates of the Democratic Front led by Enver Hoxha received 93 per cent of the votes. There was no opposition ticket but, as in Yugoslavia, facilities were provided for dissenting voters. In January 1946 the newly elected Constituent Assembly declared the formation of the Albanian People's Republic. By this time large-scale agrarian reforms had already been undertaken and the nationalisation of industry was completed in 1947.

Of all the Eastern European states, support for the communists between the wars was strongest in Bulgaria. Notwithstanding the continuous efforts of the various Bulgarian governments throughout the 1920s and 1930s to crush the organisation, the Bulgarian Communist Party was able to mount immediate resistance when the government entered the war against the Soviet Union. Initially resistance concentrated upon sabotage and on undermining the morale of the soldiers fighting with the Germans. By 1942 the communists succeeded in establishing several hundred local committees of a 'Patriotic Front' and in 1943 the 'Central Committee of the Patriotic Front' (which included representatives from the middle-class opposition) was established. With the changing fortunes of war the Bulgarian resistance movement gathered momentum. A People's Liberation Army was formed in 1943 which succeeded on 9 September 1944 (after the Red Army had crossed into Northern Bulgaria), in overthrowing the Bulgarian government. The latter was replaced by a Patriotic Front which included, in addition to the communists, representatives from the Bulgarian peasantry, the social democrats and radical middle-class parties. Nationalisation of industries and the planned collectivisation of agriculture led in the following months to a more serious struggle with conservative forces than was the case in either Yugoslavia or Albania. Nevertheless the radical policies of the Patriotic Front had the support of most of the Bulgarian population. The election to the Popular Assembly, which was postponed from August to November 1945 on the insistence of the United States and the United Kingdom (on the grounds that opposition parties had to be given time to organise), brought a clear victory for the Patriotic Front. Opposition groups within the Bulgarian Peasant and Social Democratic Parties had demanded the dissolution of the Patriotic Front, removal of communists from the ministry of the Interior and further postponement of the election. On this issue, the communist leader Georgi Dimitroff held a plebiscite in which 88 per cent of the population participated: 86 per cent of the voters supported the Patriotic Front. The opposition had boycotted the election but no irregularities were reported. The newly founded People's Assembly constituted 94 communists, 94 representatives of the peasants' league, 31 social democrats and 56 middle-class representatives. The new government continued with its programme of nationalisation, collectivisation and reconstruction of agriculture. In September 1946, 92.7 per cent of the Bulgarian electorate voted for the abolition of the monarchy and on 27 October the government held elections for the Constituent Assembly. This time the opposition united and contested the election. The result is shown in Table 1.1.

Table 1.1: Election to Bulgarian Constituent Assembly, October 1947

Parties	Vote in %	Seats	Ministers
Communists	53.8	275	10
Peasant League	12.23	69	5
Social Democrats and aligned middle-class party	3.41	18	4
Total for Patriotic Front	69.44	342	19
Opposition	28.74	99	7

The opposition parties had obviously succeeded in reducing support for the government since the November 1945 election, but 70 per cent still voted for the Patriotic Front. The opposition continued their struggle against government policies and were outlawed in April 1947 by the People's Court on the grounds of activating policies inimical to the Bulgarian people. Hence, in Bulgaria, as in Yugoslavia and Albania, the communists had enough support and were sufficiently prepared to be in a position to win the post-war domestic power struggle irrespective of the presence of Soviet troops. Only Western intervention could have brought an alternative government into power.

In Poland the situation was quite different.[10] By the summer of 1944 a complicated situation had arisen which caused considerable strain for the Soviet/Western alliance. The British-based government in exile claimed to be Poland's legitimate government. This was incompatible with the fact that at the same time Churchill — and Roosevelt — recognised the Soviet demand for an end to the *cordon sanitaire* of anti-Soviet governments around the USSR's European borders through the establishment of governments well disposed towards the USSR. The 'London Poles', who survived from the last inter-war government and who followed the same passionately anti-Soviet policies, were unlikely to maintain friendly relations with the Soviet Union. In fact their insistence upon the re-establishment of Poland's pre-war Eastern boundaries, where the Polish population was in a minority, and their claim was not buttressed by particularly strong historical justification, led to such a deterioration of relations between the Soviet Union and the 'London Poles' that the Soviet government withdrew its recognition of the latter in 1943. At the same time the resistance movement in Poland was divided between the supporters of the London government and left-

The Emergence of the New Eastern Europe (1943-7)

wing groups. While the former contained some moderate followers it also included groups of bitterly recalcitrant, anti-semitic resisters who fought the left-wing groups and later the Red Army with as much vigour as they fought the Nazis. The left resistance steadily consolidated its position among the Polish population and after the foundation of the Polish Worker Party (PPR) in 1942 (a merger of the former Communist Party with other left-wing partisan groups), the left went from strength to strength.

The crisis in Poland reached an initial peak in July 1944 when the summer offensive of the Red Army, supported by troops of the Polish left resistance, pushed the Germans behind the Curzon Line. This was followed immediately by the formation of a provisional government, the 'Polish Committee for the liberation of Poland' (PKWN). Like the People's and Patriotic Alliances in the Balkan countries, the PKWN was made up of a broad popular front. Of the 15 members, 5 belonged to the PPR, 3 to the Polish Social Democrats (PPS), and 4 to the Peasant Party (SL). There was also one democrat and two members had no party affiliation. At first – and not unexpectedly – the 'London Poles' rejected any contact or negotiation with the so-called 'Lublin government'. But as both governments tried to consolidate their position as the legal and sole government in Poland, the exiles in London were soon at a disadvantage. The Lublin government issued a manifesto which described its goal as far-reaching democratic and economic changes based on friendship with the Soviet Union. Action soon followed with a wave of substantial agrarian reforms and the nationalisation of major industries. This enabled the PKWN supporters to gain vital influence in the newly-formed 'National Councils' which, together with 'Nation's National Council (KRN), were formed in the liberated parts of Poland and held effective political power.

The London government, which soon realised that the ground was slipping from underneath its feet, decided upon a drastic and disastrous step. To present the advancing Soviets with a *fait accompli*, they called for an uprising in Warsaw to liberate the city from the Germans and establish their own government. However, they grossly underestimated the strength of the Germans, as a result of which – notwithstanding the brave fighting of the Warsaw population – the uprising was suppressed within two months. Large parts of Warsaw were levelled to the ground and 400,000 people were killed in the uprising. It is idle for Western historians to allege that the Red Army failed to assist the Warsaw uprising for opportunist political reasons. This allegation cannot be substantiated by evidence nor does it take into account that the Soviet troops were reorganising after a sustained offensive had brought them into Poland. The responsibility for this fateful step lies with the 'London Poles' and the Warsaw tragedy further undermined their position. Not surprisingly the Western governments were losing confidence in the exile government and at the Yalta conference they agreed to Soviet demands that it negotiate with the newly-formed Provisional Government which succeeded the NKVD in December 1944. The new leader of the 'London Poles', Stanislaw Mikolajczyk, realised that opposition to the Yalta agreement was futile and decided to accept an invitation to join the Provisional Government. This led to the formation of a new government, the 'government of national unity', made up of 21 members: the PPR, PPS and the Peasant Party were given six representatives, the democrats received two and one member of the government was without party affiliation. Of the six Peasant Party members, four were supporters of Mikolajczyk. Despite its promising title, the Government of National Unity was soon riven by internal strife. By mid-1945 the hard-core opposition to the popular front government had embarked upon a massive terror campaign which during 1945 alone resulted in the deaths of 3,000 communists and communist sympathisers. The extensive agrarian reforms and the nationalisation of industries were extended by the provisional government to the whole of Poland after liberation, including formerly German parts.

As Minister for Agriculture, Mikolajczyk attempted to halt the agrarian reforms and even to reverse the process. At the same time he concentrated his efforts upon winning the forthcoming elections. By undermining the democratic block of PPS, PPR and SP he tried to isolate the communists. There now was not only a ferocious underground fight against the PPR and its allies, but Mikolajczyk also set out to oust his opponents by legal means. A bitter struggle followed during which the government isolated the underground opposition and outlawed suspected collaborators. At the same time it continued the process of large-scale agrarian reform and nationalisation. The government's attempt to achieve Poland's recovery from wartime destruction was greatly aided by the acquisition of prosperous former German territories between the rivers Oder and Neisse which made new lands available for Polish peasants.

By 1946 the Democratic Front felt strong enough to give in to pressure for elections which was forthcoming from Mikolajczyk and the Western Allies. Encouraged by a massive left-wing victory in elections to a national peasants' congress, they carefully tested the ground. In June 1946 the Polish people were asked to vote in a referendum on the following three questions:

1. Do you support the abolition of the Senate?
2. Do you support the legalisation of agrarian reforms and nationalisation of key industries in a future constitution?
3. Do you support the new western border of Poland along the rivers Oder and Neisse?

Mikolajczyk had asked his supporters to vote 'No' to the first question. Of all eligible voters, 85.3 per cent participated in the plebiscite; of these, 68.2 per cent answered the first question in the affirmative – a clear setback for the opposition. To question two, 77.3 per cent answered 'Yes' and question three brought a clear 91.4 per cent vote in favour of the proposal.

The result of this was a renewed resort to underground terrorist activities by the opposition. It also sharpened the conflict between Mikolajczyk's party and the other government parties. Last-ditch efforts by the two sides to bury their differences and present a united front failed because of Mikolajczyk's absurd demand that his party be given 75 per cent of the seats in the new parliament. By now, because of his ever closer affiliation with the underground, Mikolajczyk was losing support amongst the rank and file of the Peasant Party. When the election was finally held in January 1947 the result gave the democratic block 70.1 per cent of the vote. Mikolajczyk's PSL received 10.3 per cent. A further 20 per cent went to various splinter groups.

As with most elections in which the communists gained a majority, Western political observers and historians have maintained that the result was rigged. It is true that Mikolajczyk was handicapped with the PSL being prevented from fielding candidates in some regions because their local branches were working in collaboration with the terrorist underground. No doubt there were also electoral irregularities. But there is no evidence to substantiate the claim that a 'real' election would have given the PSL a majority. As more informed Western observers and historians – who had no liking for the communist-led government – noted, the latter's active policy of reconstruction had swung the bulk of the nation behind them.[11]

The course of events in Poland clearly illustrates the basic conflicts which took place in Eastern Europe after the war. There were on the one hand the communists and their allies who, strengthened by their resistance to fascism, were determined to utilise the opportunity offered by the collapse of the old order. They were led by men hardened by underground work and persecution who had little tolerance of their political opponents and who succeeded in mobilising the nation behind their movement. They included genuine enthusiasts willing to try a radically new course. Then there were those who supported them because their section of society would gain from the change and those who assessed the situation and saw no realistic alternative. Finally, there were those who simply jumped on the bandwagon.

Opposition to the popular fronts embraced a wide section of the political spectrum: ranging from Western-orientated social democrats through conservatives to semi-fascists and fascists. The most notable opposition groups comprised social democrat reformists and liberals who attempted to establish a Western-style parliamentary democracy and hoped to transform society through parliamentary means. Most Western writers generously attribute such noble goals to the entire opposition. But there were few liberals and social democrats. The poor performance of parliamentary institutions before 1939 was by no means erased by the war. On the side of the opposition there were also conservatives who, faced with the loss of their privileged position, rallied behind anyone who looked capable of averting the socialist menace. Finally there were the remnants of semi-fascist and fascist movements which had flourished before and during the Second World War. The confrontation was fierce, with little mercy shown on either side. Nor was this to be expected in the wake of a war involving tens of millions of deaths and total national destruction.

The course of events in Romania was similar to Poland. Here, in June 1943 an anti-fascist patriotic front was formed which, as elsewhere, included the communists. By the summer of 1944 the fascist government was isolated by the Soviet advance and on 23 August an uprising in Bucharest swept Antonescu and his supporters into oblivion. In their place the King installed General Sanatescu and a multiparty government.

The next months saw heavy clashes between this 'National Democratic Block' made up of communists, social democrats and peasant parties (who demanded extensive land reforms, thorough democratisation of the state apparatus, nationalisation of banks and key industries) and their opponents from the middle class and the right wing of the labour movement. By February 1945 the situation had deteriorated so drastically that after a particularly violent clash between demonstrators and police in Bucharest the King installed a national democratic block headed by the leader of the Peasant Party, Petr Groza. Claims of gross Soviet interference in the event and of lack of popular support for the

The Emergence of the New Eastern Europe (1943-7)

Groza Government are as little supported by historical evidence as the allegation that the November elections — which saw an 88 per cent vote for the democratic block — were fraudulent.[12] The struggle over the nationalisation of industry and reconstruction of the state apparatus continued for the next year, in the process of which the monarchy was eliminated and all opposition forces ousted. In February 1948 the socialists and communists united to form the Romanian Workers' Party, which headed the 'People's Democratic Front' in the new national council to which elections were held in June 1948.

Hungary, like Romania, had been allied to Germany during the war. Compared to the other countries of Eastern and South-eastern Europe, resistance here had been modest. The communist movement, after two decades of persecution, illegality and internal division, was only beginning to recover shortly before the end of the war. With Soviet troops entering Eastern Hungary, a provisional national government was established which consisted of 71 communists, 55 members of the small peasant parties, 38 social democrats, 28 representatives from middle-class parties, 19 unionists and 19 without party affiliation. The provisional government abolished the old administrative establishment and in March 1945 introduced the first land reform in Hungary's history. With the war over, an election was held which gave the Western-orientated Peasant Party 57 per cent. The Communist Party scored 17 per cent, and the vote for the social democrats and the National Peasant Party, which were to become the 'left block' in March 1946, brought the total for the left to 41 per cent. Given the modest beginnings, this was not an inconsiderable achievement. Certainly the communists felt that they could rely on solid support in pursuit of their policies. Confrontation over land reforms and post-war economic policies occurred culminating in the spring of 1947 in the trial of members of 'Hungarian community'. This was a counter-revolutionary movement that embraced members of the Peasant Party, including the Prime Minister, Ference Nagy, and the President of the Parliament, Bela Varga. Nagy did not return from a stay in Switzerland and Varga resigned. In September 1947 a further election was held. This time the communist vote rose from 700,000 to over 1.1 million, and the Communist Party became the largest single party. The Peasant Party's support dropped from 2.7 million to 700,000. The left block now received more than 60 per cent of the votes.

By 1948 in Hungary, as in Romania and Poland, a Socialist People's Democracy had emerged. In all three countries, after a sharp conflict, the left had established itself, its success largely due to a vigorous programme and a generally widespread desire for a new radical course. The presence of Soviet troops would certainly have been a morale booster for the communists, as it would have been detrimental to the spirit of their opponents, but they did not actively interfere in the internal struggles. The Red Army did little more than guard against possible Western interference, although this was not contemplated at the time.

Czechoslovakia, unlike most of the newly formed people's republics, was relatively industrialised and urbanised. Dismemberment by the Germans and the desertion by the Allies in 1938-9 had led to a pro-Soviet feeling among all sections of the population including the middle class. This was expressed in the Benes-USSR treaty of alliance and post-war co-operation of December 1943. As elsewhere in this part of Europe, Czechoslovakia in the post-war period was governed by a national front. The active role of the communists in the post-war reconstruction led to a spectacular election success in 1946 when they scored 38 per cent of the vote. Although a communist-social democratic coalition would have commanded an absolute majority, Czechoslovakia was governed by a broad multiparty front until February 1948 when the middle-class party ministers chose the issue of police appointments for a showdown with the communists. Basically, however, the conflict was about the communists' new nationalisation proposals. On 22 February the middle-class ministers of the cabinet resigned, hoping that their social democrat colleagues would do likewise and thus force a new election. The social democrats nevertheless decided to stay in the coalition, and the communist Prime Minister Klement Gottwald declined to resign. Supported by large-scale demonstrations Gottwald asked President Benes to reappoint a new — and less conflict-ridden — ministry. The latter complied on 25 February, leaving the communists now in firm control of the new government.

The last state to join the new community of socialist countries was the German Democratic Republic in October 1949. Of all the new nations, its foundation was especially affected by international politics and by the emergence of the Cold War. Although the Allies had agreed in their final meetings towards the end of the war that Germany should stay a single political entity, notwithstanding its temporary division into four zones, the political reality after 1945 soon showed this to be an illusion. The deterioration of relations between the Soviet Union and the Western allies[13] also inevitably affected Germany. In fact the passionate anti-communist drive of President Truman enabled political interests in both Western and Soviet zones to play a role no one would have envisaged at the end of the Second World War. George Kennan, the American chargé d'affaires in Moscow, wrote as early as 1946 that unless Germany could be united on Western terms it was advisable not to leave it neutral and thus open to Soviet influence but to carry partition to its logical conclusion and 'endeavour to rescue the Western zones of Germany by walling them off against Eastern penetration and integrating them into the international pattern of Europe rather than into a united Germany'.[14]

The suggested 'walling off' took place at a rapid pace. In January 1947 the Allies established a single economic entity out of their zones. The situation was aggravated by the implementation of the Marshall Plan and its avowed but discreet aim of halting the advance of socialism. When finally on June 1948 the Western Allies announced a currency reform the Soviets retaliated by ordering a ban on all land traffic between the Western zones and Berlin. There were fears in the Soviet zone that the change in values would allow West Berliners to acquire East Berlin's supplies of goods at artificially low prices. Next day the Soviets announced their currency reform while the blockade continued. The Berlin Blockade, the first major crisis of the Cold War, lasted for ten months until April 1949. The Soviet leadership had hoped to prevent the formation of a pro-West, and hence anti-Soviet West Germany. A neutral Germany — even if this meant a non-socialist Germany — seems to have been a persistent part of Stalin's policies until his death in 1953. If this was his aim, it failed. On 23 May the Federal Republic of Germany was proclaimed by Dr Konrad Adenauer who became its first chancellor. Events in the Soviet zone now followed suit. Elections were held for a People's Congress and on 7 October 1949 the German People's Council, elected by the Congress, proclaimed the foundation of the German Democratic Republic.

Notwithstanding the strong influence of the international situation, it would be mistaken to explain the foundation of the GDR as a mere side product of the Cold War. Some of the events in the Soviet zone of Germany after the Second World War were not unlike developments in the other socialist republics. The union of the social democrats with the communists in 1946 was certainly a commendable step after the division of the inter-war years and the failure of a disunited German labour movement to thwart the advance of National Socialism. The newly-founded SED (Socialist Unity Party), which gained the support of about half the population in a series of local and regional elections held in 1946, pursued a programme of land reform and nationalisation. The heavy German war reparations to the Soviet Union, which were met almost solely by the Soviet zone at a time when the United States was already pumping money into the exhausted Western zones, caused considerable economic difficulties. The long standing anti-Soviet tradition among most Germans, which was aggravated by the loss of German territory to Poland and the Soviet Union, added to the difficulties for the new government. Nevertheless in the GDR too there was a wave of enthusiastic support among many people who felt that they were at the threshold of a new stage in history.

The abysmal record of the pre-war years, the disillusionment with the West and the traumatic war years had led to radical left-wing governments in Eastern Europe. After the fascist disaster, positive expectations for the future were widely held throughout Eastern Europe in 1948. Nevertheless the new course did not prove as smooth as many in their post-war idealism hoped.

Notes and References

1. Fritz Fischer, *Germany's Aim in the First World War* (Chatto and Windus, 1967), also *War of Illusions* (1975); J. Moses, *The War Aims of Imperial Germany* (Queensland University Press, Brisbane, 1968), also *The Politics of Illusion: The Fischer Controversy in German Historiography* (Prior, London, 1975).
2. Eastern Europe in this book is used as a political expression. Geographically it includes Eastern Europe as well as the Balkans.
3. J. Joll, *Europe Since 1870* (Harmondsworth: Penguin, 1976), p. 296.
4. Ivan T. Berend and G. Ranki, *Economic Development in East Central Europe* (Columbia University Press, New York, 1974), p. 284.
5. Ibid., p. 287.
6. Ibid., p. 290.
7. Ibid., p. 318.
8. R.V. Burks, *The Dynamics of Communism in Eastern Europe* (Princeton University Press, New Jersey, 1961), Appendix A.
9. Klaus Böllinger, *Weltgeschehen 1945-1966* (Deutscher Verlag der Wissenschaften, 1967), p. 264.
10. For a detailed account and documents note B. Drukier and A. Polonsky, *The Beginning of Communist Rule in Poland* (Routledge and Kegan Paul, London, 1980).
11. O. Forst de Battaglia, *Zwischeneuropa* (1953), p. 99; W. Woods, *Poland: Eagles in the East* (London, 1969), pp. 117-20.
12. Most accounts of the post-war struggle in Romania are based on a book by Reuben H. Markham, an American journalist, called *Rumania Under the Soviet Yoke* (Boston, 1949). A simplistic Cold War account, it is based entirely on the view from the windows of Western embassies. As even H. Seton-Watson points out in a recent essay, this was not a particularly well-placed position to arrive at sober judgements, 'Thirty Years After' in M. McCauley, *Communist Power*, pp. 223-4.
13. For a more recent publication about the Cold War: C.S. Maier, *Origins of the Cold War and Contemporary Europe* (New Viewpoints, New York, 1978).
14. Quoted in Jonathan Steele, *Socialism with a German Face* (Cape, London, 1977), pp. 36-7.

2 PLANNED ECONOMY AND COLD WAR (1948-53)

Not only in terms of the loss of human life but also in terms of direct economic devastation, Eastern Europe suffered most severely from the Second World War. In Poland every village, town and city was affected. Twenty-five per cent of the farmsteads were totally devastated. It is estimated that either through destruction or confiscation Poland lost 43 per cent of its horses, 60 per cent of its cattle and 78 per cent of its pigs. In Warsaw more than two-thirds of the buildings were destroyed or severely damaged. Yugoslavia and Hungary too were deprived of more than half of their livestock and the losses in eastern Slovenia amounted to 80 per cent of the total. Destruction of the transport system and industries was no less staggering. Throughout the region during their retreat the Germans destroyed bridges, rendered railways and waterways useless and confiscated the bulk of locomotives, rolling stock and barges. The total material damage in Poland was estimated at 18.2 billion US dollars. Losses in most of the other Eastern European countries were comparable. The refugee appeared as an additional problem and the transfer of minorities involved shifting and resettling millions of people — eight million in Poland alone.

With the damage to crops and livestock, food production fell far below pre-war levels. Thus the end of the war coincided with a severe famine throughout Eastern and South-eastern Europe. For the first two post-war years the surmounting of this food problem became the chief priority. Extensive land reforms were carried out by the popular front governments in all countries. The Polish land reform of September 1944 redistributed more than one million hectares of land from former large states to 379,000 new settlers. After the German collapse 5.5 million Poles were settled in the former German territories. In Hungary the state confiscated and redistributed three and a quarter million hectares. Romania redistributed more than a million hectares and in Yugoslavia 542,000 hectares of former German holdings were given to Yugoslavian cultivators. Nevertheless, soil exhaustion coupled with bad weather prevented improvements in output during the immediate post-war years. Some aid was provided by the newly-founded United Nations Relief and Rehabilitation Administration (UNRRA) but during the latter's short period of operation the steps undertaken were ineffective in view of the magnitude of the problem. Only Poland and Yugoslavia received substantial aid. Hence, not surprisingly, after the impact of the war and the subsequent famine, the anticipation by many Western observers that the radical political shift would be accompanied by equally drastic economic and social changes soon proved to be correct. Within three years all countries of the region with the exception of the Soviet zone of Germany (later the German Democratic Republic) experienced an initial implementation of the planned economy.

'The object of the Plan' wrote an enthusiastic observer in the early 1950s, 'is to introduce order, to raise the standard of living, to end agrarian poverty, industrial backwardness and unemployment. The Plan seeks a balanced economy [with] a due proportion between industry and agriculture. The Plan seeks freedom from the position of colonial status. The Plan seeks national independence, with wider instalments of economic equality. The means thereto is the raising of the productivity of labour, together with the lessening of its burden.'[1] As these lines of the then Dean of Canterbury, Hewlett Johnson, indicate, the economic plan was intended to ensure that production was for the needs of the whole population: to supply men and women with the goods and services they required for everyday life, food, clothing, housing, education, health, transport, recreation and other essentials.

The system of planned economy originated in the Soviet Union during the 1920s. To paraphrase, the plan defines the basic economic parameters, rates and directions, such as the rate of growth of national product and the proportion of capital formation and the relative size and composition of public and private consumption. It determines the size and pattern of productive capacities and of outputs. Ideally, planned economy is based on the interactive consultation of the planning authorities with all sections of the community to formulate the targets for the allocation of national resources between investment, government and personal consumption. In theory centralised planning permits a more rational management of the economy, to utilise and enhance the investment, manpower, industrial equipment and natural resources of a country in the most effective manner towards the constant goal of raising the standard of living of the people. Admittedly, and in this respect not unlike the Western market economy, a considerable discrepancy emerged between the theory and the more sombre reality of the practice. Or, as one observer remarked, 'life has revealed its limitations'.[2] Nevertheless the indubitably impressive industrial success of the Soviet Union, the fact that this nation, having started from a position of rural backwardness and almost complete industrial chaos after war and civil war, was capable by the 1940s of virtually defeating the powerful German war machinery single-handedly, made the Soviet model attractive. The Soviet experience was especially attractive for countries which, starting from a position of industrial backwardness, wished to embark upon a programme of rapid economic growth. This feeling existed irrespective of the situation in which Eastern Europe had been effectively liberated from Nazism by the army of the Soviet Union.

The initial short-term plans were based on a mixture of nationalised industry in respect of large-scale undertakings with the retention of a still considerable private sector and had the primary aim of restoring production to pre-war levels. The first country to implement such a policy was Poland. The redistribution of land and large-scale nationalisation of industry met opposition. Nevertheless, the new economic course was established relatively smoothly. Even before the war state ownership of industry in Poland was amongst the most extensive in Europe outside the Soviet Union. As in most of Europe the state owned the transport system and in addition held 100 per cent of the chemical industry, 70 per cent of the steel industry and 50 per cent of the metal production. The practical elimination of Poland's bourgeoisie during the war and German ownership of much of Poland's industry effectively removed the remaining obstacles to a substantial extension of nationalisation, which was officially decreed on 3 January 1946. Under this law the state took over mining, the petroleum industry, power, gas and water works, synthetic fuel production, ferrous and non-ferrous metals, foundries, armament industries, collieries, sugar refineries, industrial alcohol distilleries and breweries, yeast factories, flour mills of above a certain capacity, cold storage facilities and printing establishments, as well as any other undertakings 'capable of employing more than 50 workers per shift'.

The Polish nationalisation measures effectively left almost half of all plants employing five or more workers within the private sector although the public sector of industry employed 86.8 per cent of the total workforce compared to only 10 per cent in private industry. This was the basis upon which the government, on 21 September 1946, initiated the first three-year plan. To reach its overall target of lifting the standard of living of the working population above pre-war levels, the plan specified five major aims; first, to strengthen the new order and prepare for the transformation of the country's socio-economic structure; secondly, to overcome the destruction resulting from the war; thirdly, to integrate the territory acquired in the West and North; and fourthly, to increase Poland's share of world trade. The plan also set out to encourage those Poles who had left, or were forced to leave the country to return and finally to lower the cost of production of goods and services. This first plan, in contrast to the subsequent longer-term plans, in its initial stages emphasised consumer before capital goods. However, the plan soon faced difficulties, especially in the rural sector. Food production was curtailed by the severe winter of 1946-7, followed by large-scale springtime floods and a summer drought. Moreover, the integration of the new Western provinces into Poland posed difficulties, although once resettlement was completed the resources of the highly industrialised parts of Silesia proved a considerable asset. Overall, the target of the three-year plan was reached. Despite setbacks, the rate of industrial growth was spectacular and, in 1949, on completion of the plan Polish industry employed twice as many people as in 1939.

In Czechoslovakia the first move towards a planned economy was not as vigorous. The nationalisation laws of October 1945 covered the remaining power stations that did not serve non-nationalised industries; iron and steel works and rolling mills; all non-ferrous metal works except those which were economically independent and not included in a combine or trust; foundries with more than 400 employees; electrical and other engineering works; optical and precision works with more than 500 workers; armaments and munitions plants; chemical plants with more than 150 employees; various categories of glass production; stone, clay and ceramic undertakings with over 150 employees; brick-making enterprises with over 200 employees; pulp and paper manufacturers with over 300 employees; silk enterprises with over 150 workers; saw mills and mills producing semi-manufactured wood products with over 300 employees; textile-spinning mills with over 400 employees; textile-weaving mills with 500 workers; plants for textile printing with over 200 employees; clothing factories with over 500 employees; tanning and leather manufacturers with over 400 employees; all gramophone-record producers; sugar mills and refineries; alcohol distilleries and breweries with specified capacities; and chocolate and oleomargarine plants with over 500 employees. This law nationalised 16.4 per cent of all enterprises employing 61.2 per cent of all industrial workers. It left 50 per cent of the textile industry in private hands, 50 per cent of the paper manufacturing industry, 42 per cent of the leather industry and 85 per cent of the foodstuff industry. Like Poland, Czechoslovakia commenced its first short-term plan in 1947, although the latter's duration was only two years. The Czechoslovakian plan also attempted to overcome wartime damage and restore pre-war levels of industrial and agricultural production, a goal which was not altogether achieved. In particular those industries that were still largely in private hands fell short of the plan's production targets: a factor which contributed significantly to the February 1948 confrontation and the more drastic nationalisation laws of that year.

Yugoslavia was the only country in the socialist block which embarked on an immediate long-term plan without going through the preparatory process of establishing term targets. However, confrontation between the Yugoslav Communist Party and the other socialist governments of Eastern Europe, which led to the expulsion of the former from the Comintern in July 1948, ensured that a Soviet-style planned economy never emerged in that country.

The nations which had been fighting on the side of the fascist powers evinced a slower start to nationalisation and a planned economy. In contrast to the former Allied countries the traditional social structure in Bulgaria, Romania and Hungary was not so radically altered in the short term, and a further hindrance, especially in the case of Romania and Hungary, was the issue of reparation payments to the Soviet Union. Bulgaria was the first ex-enemy country to nationalise its industry and implement a two-year plan, in 1947. The nationalisation law of December 1947 brought 85.3 per cent of industrial output within the state sector leaving a private sector of 6 per cent and a mixed sector of 9 per cent. In Hungary the pace was much slower. As late as mid-1947 the state sector contained a total of only 32 per cent of the employment in manufacture. This had risen to between 40 and 50 per cent by the end of 1947. The first three-year plan commencing in 1947 initially resembled more the plans of Western Labourite governments in the immediate post-war period than the Soviet model or the subsequent five-year plans. It merely outlined the proposed general development of production and initiated some investment projects of outstanding importance. The overall difficulty of post-war reconstruction was initially aggravated by reparation payments to the Soviet Union. Hungary had been obliged to deliver goods worth US$ 200 million over a period of 18 years, but the Soviet Union repeatedly reduced these reparation payments and in addition sent considerable technical and material aid to the former enemy state. The Soviets also sold trucks and tractors to Hungary at prices far below prevailing world prices. Contrary to frequent claims by Western writers, the reparations actually paid stood in no relation to the damage done by the Hungarian Army in the Western USSR during 1941-2.

Romanian reparation payments were originally fixed at US$ 300 million. This sum too was reduced considerably over subsequent years.

By 1945 the Soviets had already returned rolling stock together with some of the industrial equipment they had been operating and granted the Romanians a loan of 300,000 tons of grain. There was no major nationalisation drive in Romania until the end of 1947 and the country did not start its reconstruction plans until the end of 1948. Then the planning consisted only of two one-year plans covering the period to the end of 1950.

The initial drive towards socialisation throughout the region proceeded slowly. In assessing the economic future of Eastern and Southeastern Europe, a contemporary American observer, P.N. Rosenstein-Rodan wrote in 1943 that the states in this region had two options in respect of industrialisation. They could modernise on their own, on the 'Russian model' aiming at self-sufficiency without relying upon foreign investment. This would necessitate the bringing into being of every stage of industry, heavy as well as light industry, with the final result being a 'national economy built like a vertical industrial concern'.[3] According to Rosenstein-Rodan this path would suffer 'grave disadvantages' because the necessary capital could only be raised internally at the expense of the standard of living of the people. This approach, as he put it: 'implies a heavy and in our opinion unnecessary sacrifice'. The alternative would integrate Eastern Europe into the world economy, based on the international division of labour and would ultimately produce more wealth for everybody. With hindsight the historian today may well question the assumption that large-scale Western capitalist investment is a benefit to developing countries. In the 1940s, however, only the first alternative was open to the states of Eastern Europe as a consequence of the deterioration of East-West relations.

There is a flourishing literature on the subject of the Cold War which continues to proliferate. Traditional Western historians and political observers have always maintained that the United States government had to take up an increasingly strong stand after the Second World War to halt Soviet expansionism.[4] This argument has been challenged throughout the 1960s and early 1970s in the wake of the 'soul-searching' or re-evaluation of the Western position in international relations which accompanied the Vietnam disaster. A group of academics normally referred to as the 'New Left' or the 'Radical School' presented the view that the Truman administration after the Second World War revived traditional anti-left policies in the United States. These were directed not only against the Soviet Union and communism but also against any form of left-wing political development which threatened the economic interest of the United States. Not surprisingly this radical interpretation

Planned Economy and Cold War (1948-53)

has been severely criticised by the Western academic establishment, although some of the former's arguments are buttressed by substantial evidence. Given the political and social incompatability of the two systems, the ground for compromise and co-operation was certainly thin. The Alliance held, notwithstanding considerable strain, as long as there was a common enemy. But the defeat of Germany and Japan removed the basis for future mutual understanding. The Truman administration lost no time in dismantling Roosevelt's approach of carefully nurturing the United States-Soviet relationship. As early as January 1946 he urged the Secretary of State James F. Byrnes to stop 'babying the Soviets' and present 'an iron fist and strong language'.[5] The word 'iron' subsequently acquired a certain popularity among Western conservatives. Three months later the former British Prime Minister Winston Churchill delivered his famous speech at Fulton, Missouri. Churchill demanded that the United States and Britain form a grand alliance to deal with the Soviets from a position of overwhelming strength. He praised the Anglo-American atomic monopoly and demanded the creation of a United Nations force. This would enable the West to come to terms with Russia and create settlements based on 'good understanding'. The most memorable aspect of his speech was, of course, the classic phrase that from 'Stettin in the Baltic to Trieste in the Adriatic, an iron curtain has descended across the continent'. In the remainder of continental Europe too, he claimed that the communists were undermining the political structure. This speech certainly caused embarrassment for the British Labour Government. It was also inaccurate and politically confused. The strength of the communists in Western Europe arose from their role in the resistance movement and in 1946 East-West border regulations were still comparatively unrestricted. As an entirely anti-Soviet manifesto, it further worsened East-West relations. At the same time the dispatches of the Moscow chargé d'affaires, George F. Kennan, with their elaborate and imaginative outlines of Soviet imperialist grand strategies, did little to defuse the situation. Nor did the reports of the United States ambassador W. Averall Harriman, which feature so prominently in the works of Western diplomatic historians, provide any elements of enlightenment. These men were leading Western public servants, trained in the conservative tradition of American diplomacy who, although no doubt acting from honest motives, were scarcely in a position to assess objectively the complicated situation of post-war Eastern Europe. From their perspective the political spectrum was confined at its extreme to left liberalism or Western social democratic labourism; beyond this the political scene was submerged in a uniform sea of red. Out of this background the Truman administration officially announced its 'containment policies' in 1947 and the Cold War confrontation was to reach its first climax in 1948 with the implementation of the Marshall Plan.

The Marshall Plan has been almost universally viewed in a favourable light. It was seen as an act of unprecedented generosity for the United States to contribute so magnanimously to the rebuilding of the economies of its potential competitors and to distribute American goods for the relief of the war-torn nations of Europe. A recent publication by the British historians, Sir John Wheeler-Bennett and Anthony Nicholls, states that the Marshall Plan 'will surely be recorded as one of America's greatest contributions to the peace of the world'.[6] In effect the Marshall Plan was an act of enlightened self-interest which had the objective of forestalling communist penetration by raising European living standards and re-establishing normal trading relations for mutual benefit. It also served to assist American industry in the transition from war- to peacetime production by providing export outlets in Europe. To the great concern of the British and French governments, who feared that their share would consequently be considerably reduced, the offer of aid included the Soviet Union and the Eastern European states. Given the latter's desperate economic situation, great hopes were placed upon American aid. The Soviet Foreign Minister Molotov arrived in Paris, where the US programme was to be discussed, with 89 technicians and academics. However, the negotiations broke down over the issue of how the plan was to be administered. The Western insistence upon an integrated plan for the whole of Europe was unacceptable to the Soviets as this would have meant integrating the USSR and its new socialist neighbours into the capitalist economic sphere, placing its economy under the guidance of the United States and its Western European allies. Not surprisingly the Soviet Union demanded the withdrawal of its allies from the Marshall programme.

The overall situation in 1948 was further aggravated in the March of that year by the Berlin crisis. The latter was sparked off by the decision of the three Western occupying powers of Germany to introduce a currency reform in their zones, without previous consultation with the Soviets. In response the Soviets ordered a ban on all land traffic between the Western zones and Berlin. The blockade of West Berlin lasted for 13 months and is generally regarded as the high point of the Cold War and the low point of East-West relations. Thus by the end of 1948 the people's republics had necessarily to make their own way without Western assistance. Whether the West, especially the United States, ever seriously considered large-scale aid to the East is doubtful. Recent publications by Western writers who do not occupy a new-left or anti-west position throw doubt on American plans for large-scale aid to Eastern Europe. Writings on post-war Czechoslovakia maintain that the United States government had by and large written off that country by the autumn of 1948.[7] They point to a discrepancy between rhetorical demands for the establishment of Western-style governments which were in no way backed by realistic action in practice.

Unlike the introductory short-term plans, the first long-term plans were far-reaching and ambitious. Emphasis in all of them was on the rapid development of the heavy industrial sector. Czechoslovakia and Bulgaria began their first five-year plans in 1949. The Czechoslovakian five-year plan initially attempted to raise industrial production by 57 per cent with particular emphasis being placed upon the metal industry which was designated to expand by some 70 per cent. These figures were later raised to 70 and 130 per cent respectively. Heavy machinery was the leading item with a planned growth rate of 200-300 per cent. To catch up with the already industrially advanced Czechs, the Slovakian growth rate was supposed to be 20 per cent above the former. Production in the rural sector was to increase by 37 per cent and it was hoped to raise the overall standard of living by 35 per cent. The first Bulgarian plan also hoped to double the 1939 national income. Forty per cent of investment was scheduled for industry, 22 per cent for transport, 17.8 per cent for agriculture and 20 per cent for social services and culture. The Hungarian plan which started in 1950 was even more ambitious. National income was to increase by 63 per cent, industrial production by 86 per cent, production of heavy industry by 104 per cent and agricultural output by 42 per cent. The standard of living was predicted to rise by 35 per cent. After one year these figures were further raised. The projected increase in the production of heavy industry was now 280-290 per cent. The increase in national income was now to be 120-140 per cent and the standard of living was to rise by 50-55 per cent in comparison to 1949.

Poland and Romania began their first long-term plans in 1951 with similar targets. These first plans undoubtedly encouraged rapid industrial development and an economic growth rate which compared favourably to Western Europe at that time. Nevertheless, after a boisterous start a series of difficulties emerged which in part stemmed from inexperience in economic planning, through excessive, over-ambitious objectives or through outright neglect. It soon became evident, for example, that the supply of metal ores could not keep up with industrial demand. The readjusted target figures of the early 1950s proved unrealistic and also the relative neglect of the agricultural sector and of consumer goods began to have its effect upon the population. However, before this problem reached even more drastic proportions, in the final stages of the first five-year plans the political situation began to enter a dark phase.

Referring to the late 1940s and early 1950s, Eastern European historians limit themselves to the admission that the 'erroneous interpretation of the proletarian dictatorship in the years of the personality cult' led to grave distortions of Marxist-Leninist principles. Using the more direct language of Western historians, the British economic historian, Alec Nove, puts it more bluntly when claiming that anyone trying to defend Stalin in his last years would have to plead insanity. With the state of the Cold War having further deteriorated with the Berlin crisis, the Marshall Plan and the continuing United States nuclear supremacy, the final break between the Soviet leadership and Tito could not have come at a worse time. Yugoslav-Soviet relations began to deteriorate during 1947 with disagreements over Yugoslav economic and military policies. The crisis reached a first peak in March 1947 when the Soviet Union withdrew its military and economic advisers and in July the Cominform expelled Yugoslavia on the grounds of anti-Soviet policies. To quote the manifesto, 'the leaders of the Communist Party of Yugoslavia have taken a stand unworthy of Communists and have begun to identify the foreign policy of the Soviet Union with the foreign policy of the imperialist powers . . . Instead of honestly accepting this criticism and taking the Bolshevist path of correcting these mistakes, the leaders of the Communist Party of Yugoslavia, suffering from boundless ambition, arrogance and conceit met this criticism with belligerence and hostility.'[8] The expulsion was accompanied by a fierce press campaign in the other Eastern European states which denounced the 'fascist and nationalist clique around Tito' as 'agents of the Imperialist Reaction', and further alleging that the Yugoslav Communist Party was in the hands of murderers and spies, of Yugoslav mercenaries of capitalism.

The hapless state of affairs brought about by anti-Titoism reached its low point with the Slansky trials in Prague. Commencing on 22 November 1952, to the stunned amazement of the Czech people and Western observers who listened to the broadcasts of the trials, the former Secretary General of the Czech Communist Party and other leading Czech and Slovak communists levelled the most atrocious accusations against themselves, admitting the gravest crimes against their country and the cause of international socialism. The trials, which were modelled on Stalin's show trials of the 1930s, followed the well-known pattern. The defendants all acknowledged their guilt and accepted the sentences as being just. There were, however, a few nuances. One of the defendants, the former *Rude Pravo* journalist Simone-Katz, demanded in almost hysterical exuberance that hanging was the only just sentence for him. The son of Frejka, another defendant, implored the courts to grant him the favour of allowing him to express his contempt of his father before the latter was executed. The wife of the former Vice Premier London demanded in her name and in the name of their three young children, whom she was to raise as good communists, that the father of the family be dealt with in the harshest fashion. In addition to this there were thousands of letters, telegrams and resolutions held at hundreds of meetings of workers throughout the country which insisted that the traitors be punished for their crimes. The damage done by the anti-Tito Slansky trials can never be repaired, although it must be noted, if for no other reason than accuracy, that anti-Titoism did not reach Czechoslovakian proportions in the other countries. In Hungary the former Foreign Minister, Laszlo Rajk, was executed after having been found guilty of the charge of conspiring with the Yugoslavs. The evidence in this case was also fabricated. In Poland the former Secretary General Gomulka and his associates were removed from office and were for a time imprisoned. In Romania, the grand old lady of Romanian communism, Anna Pauker, and her associates were expelled from their leading role in the party and in the GDR too, anti-Titoism meant expulsion for some party members from their leading positions.

It is reported that when the news of Stalin's death reached the outside world on 6 March 1953, many people in the Soviet Union and the people's democracies collapsed in tears for, as a dissident Soviet observer grudgingly conceded, the despot was widely popular.[9] The tears of his pious supporters notwithstanding, by the time of Stalin's death in early spring 1953 a great deal of the elan of the new course, which was so inspiring in the immediate post-war years, had lapsed. In several countries serious economic and political problems had arisen which were not overcome by the time of Stalin's death.

Notes and References

1. Hewlett Johnson, *Eastern Europe in the Socialist World* (Lawrence and Wishart, London, 1955), p. 35.
2. Alfred Zaubermann, *Industrial Progress in Poland, Czechoslovakia and East Germany 1937-1962* (Oxford University Press, London, 1964), p. 4.

3. P.N. Rosenstein-Rodan, 'Problems of Industrialisation of Eastern and South-Eastern Europe', *The Economic Journal*, vol. LIII (1943), p. 107; quoted in N. Spulber, *The Economics of Communist Eastern Europe* (London, 1957), p. 286.

4. For a most recent discussion of the Cold War: C.S. Maier (ed.), *The Origins of the Cold War and Contemporary Europe* (New York/London, 1978), ch. 1.

5. Gabriel Kolko, *The Limits of Power* (Harper and Row, New York, 1972), p. 32.

6. Sir John Wheeler-Bennett and Anthony Nicholls, *The Semblance of Peace: Political Settlement After The Second World War* (Macmillan, London, 1974), p. 575.

7. Daniel Yergin, 'The Origins of the Cold War and the National Security of the State' in C.S. Maier (ed.), *The Origins of the Cold War, op. cit.*

8. F. Roy Willis, *Europe in the Global Age: 1939 to the Present* (Dodd, Mead and Co.), p. 240.

9. François Fejtö, *A History of the People's Democracies* (Pall Mall Press, London, 1971), p. 17.

3 CONFRONTATION AND CONSOLIDATION (1954-9)

By the early 1950s the people's republics had made an enormous effort to change their societies from a condition of agrarian backwardness to modern industrialisation. With the partial exception of the GDR and Czechoslovakia before the war, their economies at that time were backward, largely dependent on agriculture. Per capita income had been low and unemployment had been high. The region had functioned as a reservoir of cheap food and raw materials for the industrialised capitalist countries and a dumping ground for their manufactures. After 1947 the people's republics faced the additional problem of the Western embargo on exports of advanced industrial equipment to the region.

Consequently, the policies of the new governments of promoting rapid industrialisation met with widespread popular support. The key to industrial growth lay in the speedy establishment of a strong heavy industrial sector and there was no disagreement that the major effort in the first long-term plans should be directed towards this goal. It seems, however, that to varying degrees the new leadership and the economic planners lost sight of what was possible and practicable. The initial target figures for heavy industry everywhere were higher than for any other branch of the economy and were unrelated to the resources available at the time, a problem which in some countries was further aggravated by the subsequent increases of the initial plan targets to even more unrealistic levels. This latter step further worsened the position of the agricultural sector and of the light and consumer industries.

The planned intention to raise agricultural output failed for a variety of reasons. To begin with, the formation of agricultural producers' co-operatives proved a difficult process. Throughout the people's republics four types of co-operatives were created. In the first type there was private ownership of land, draught animals, implements and crops but communal labour. The second type consisted of collective ploughing and sowing of the arable land but with individual reaping. The costs of ploughing and sowing were shared by each member according to the land contributed and members kept the returns after the deduction of these costs. The third type of producers' co-operatives comprised collectivised ploughing, sowing, harvesting and threshing. Profit was distributed after cost deduction according to the land and area, draught animals and implements contributed. Finally, there was the so-called *kolkhoz* type where both the land and means of cultivation were common property, with each member being paid according to work units. This new agricultural policy was met with considerable suspicion by the rural population and the methods used in persuading the farm owners to join the co-operatives often exceeded the 'voluntarist' principle. In addition to this, the heavy taxes and compulsory requisitioning of products placed upon the larger Kulak-type farms forced many cultivators to abandon their property, which in turn led to vast areas of land being left fallow. The production of modern machinery which was hoped to aid the process of increasing agricultural output fell behind expectations. All these factors ensured that food production in the early 1950s remained low, which in turn resulted in a lowering of the standard of living. At the same time construction of new dwellings in industrial centres was inadequate in relation to the expansion of the workforce brought about by the plan. The general neglect of consumer goods in the first long-term plans further aggravated the situation. There were shortages in all the basic requirements of everyday life, a fact which the political leaders failed to realise for a long time. It is thus not surprising that discontent grew amongst the people.

The first signs of disaffection in Eastern Europe emerged in Czechoslovakia. In addition to the perpetual problem of food distribution, this country suffered from a severe winter in 1952-3. Lack of heating fuel due to the demands of heavy industry enhanced the degree of discontent. To deal with these economic problems the Czechoslovakian government decided to introduce a drastic currency reform, which involved a lowering of the value of the Krona on the international money market to one eighth of its previous value. This not only affected the savings of those middle-class citizens who, despite the government's socialist policies, had managed 'to put a little aside' but also further reduced the purchasing power for almost the whole of the Czechoslovakian workforce.

To add salt to the wounds the government decided, on the day the currency law became effective, to introduce a law which asserted an 'unlimited duty to work' in case of 'economic emergency'. What constituted an 'economic emergency' was not spelt out but the coupling of further cuts in the standard of living with the possibility of increased working hours was the straw that broke the camel's back. Old party comrades from all over the country protested and in several communist strongholds the workers took even stronger action. There were strikes in the coal-mining region of Moravia and around Plzen and demonstrations

Confrontation and Consolidation (1954-9)

in Moravia-Ostrova and Opava. In some places pictures of Stalin and President Gottwald were destroyed and the unrest did not settle until the government, under pressure from the unions, decided to withdraw the emergency decrees. The protest surprised not only the Czechoslovakian party leadership — it also virtually escaped Western comment, although the latter is normally very quick to publicise instances of unrest 'behind the Iron Curtain'. The Western press, however, got its sensation two weeks later, when a far more spectacular protest occurred right in Berlin.

None of the newly-formed people's republics faced difficulties to the extent of the German Democratic Republic. The post-war situation effectively curtailed access to its Western sources of raw materials and its Western markets for semi-manufactured goods, a fact which could not be remedied immediately by the opening up of trading links with its new partners in Eastern and South-eastern Europe. Wartime destruction in that part of Germany which became the Soviet zone after the war was considerably greater than in the Western zones. Only a fraction of Germany's pre-war natural resources had been located there and, to reiterate, reparation payments to the Soviet Union were almost solely extracted from the Soviet zone. Altogether 45 per cent of industrial plant, 70 per cent of electricity-generating capacity, 50 per cent of urban housing stock and 30 per cent of the agricultural machinery had been destroyed or rendered useless. The Nazi Wehrmacht had scuttled 2,000 barges and blown up 5,000 railway and 4,500 road bridges. Four obsolete blast furnaces were the entire potential for metallurgy production left in that part of the country. In the Western part of the former German Reich, notably in the Ruhr, 120 blast furnaces were still functioning. Seventy per cent of the industrial potential existing in 1945 on the territory of what was later to become the German Democratic Republic (GDR) and the Federal Republic of Germany fell to the share of the FRG, of which 20 per cent had been destroyed. A mere 30 per cent was located in the GDR, of which 45 per cent was destroyed. As a consequence, the GDR had almost no iron and steel industry and no coal and iron ore mining worth mentioning at the time it was founded. On the other hand, numerous enterprises in the metal-working industries of the GDR had been dependent on iron and steel supplies from the West.

Efficient deep-sea ports did not exist nor was there any ship-building industry worthy of note. Both, however, were badly needed for the development of foreign trade. The German Democratic Republic also had almost no natural resources, with the exception of lignite and potash salts. In addition to this there was the huge population movement from the former parts of Germany incorporated into Poland and the Soviet Union and of the so-called *Volksdeutsche* who had been expelled from their homelands in South-eastern Europe. This added 3½ million people to the population of the Soviet zone. Then, as the West German recovery began to surge ahead and produce rising living standards, the steady flow of people from East Germany to the West commenced. This was to cripple the economic and political life of the GDR for its first twelve years.

The government of the Federal Republic, which claimed to be the sole representative of the German people and which dismissed the GDR as a bastard creation of Joseph Stalin, did its share further to torpedo the struggling GDR economy by abolishing trading connections in respect of a wide range of vital sectors of industry. In fact the Federal Republic's economic policies were so effective that in 1952, in anticipation of an impending collapse of the GDR economy, the West German government set up a so-called 'Research Council for Questions of Germany's Reunification' (*Forschungsbeirat für Fragen der Wiedervereinigung Deutschlands*), which was charged with the task of planning the reversal of the socialist policies introduced in the GDR as a preliminary for its integration with the Federal Republic. As one GDR historian remarked: 'the same people who shed big crocodile tears about the suffering brothers and sisters in the East left no stone unturned to strangle the economy of the other country'.[1]

Under such difficult circumstances there were adequate grounds to pursue a more qualified version of the heavy industry programme on the lines of the Soviet model. However, the first GDR Socialist Unity Party (SED) leader Walter Ulbricht, a staunch old communist and an ardent admirer of the Soviet model, would have nothing of moderation. Consequently throughout the early 1950s there was an inadequate supply of basic essentials in relation to the needs of the population. Under these circumstances the decision of the SED leadership in mid-1952 to raise the output of heavy industry at the expense of consumer goods and, at the same time, introduce several measures to weaken further the position of the middle class and the rural community led to a considerable increase in the number of people leaving the republic during the first months of 1953. To cope with the continuing deterioration of the economic situation it was finally announced during the May Day demonstration of 1953 that the work norms were to be raised by 10 per cent. At this point it became obvious that there was considerable opposition within the SED leadership to such a tough course and this seems to have been shared by members of the Soviet leadership. This opposition gained the upper hand and on 11 June 1953 the GDR national newspaper published a new programme, which reduced investment in heavy industry and aimed to step up production of consumer goods. The new programme also lifted a number of taxes on farmers, craftsmen, shopkeepers and private firms. The latter especially were to be given a new lease of life through the government's invitation to those citizens who had gone to the West to return and by the offer of economic assistance. Farmers too were promised money, machines and seeds. Discrimination against the Church and other sections of the middle class was to cease and the latter were to have their ration cards returned. Finally, a number of recent price increases were revoked.

From the available material it is difficult to judge why a demonstration of building workers occurred on 16 June 1953. Western accounts maintain that the work norms had not been reduced and that, in consequence, building workers marched to Council of Ministers to make that demand. GDR historians, on the other hand, claim that the workers marched unaware that the norms had in fact been reduced and that a great deal of the ill will was fomented by Western agents. The following day there were confrontations and protest marches in several parts of the country, which involved between 300,000-370,000 workers. In Berlin, rioting and looting took place.

In his recent book on the GDR, the British journalist Jonathan Steele correctly states that the events of 16 and 17 June have since become a casualty of Cold War propaganda. 'In the West', writes Steele, '... the conventional wisdom is that a countrywide popular uprising for reunification on the Western model was suppressed by Soviet tanks. June 17 has become national day in the Federal Republic, an occasion for anticommunist fervour and sanctimonious speeches of concern by politicians for "our oppressed brothers and sisters on the other side".'[2] (However, since the days of the Brandt Government these occasions have ceased to be utilised for such propaganda purposes.) On the other hand, Steele also takes issue with the GDR account of the event, in allowing for an element of spontaneity on the part of the workers rather than blaming the whole affair on manipulation by the Federal Republic. However, Steele does admit that a number of Western agencies were involved and that by the time the Soviet tanks arrived the vigour had gone out of the protest. Most of the workers had already dispersed. There certainly is little evidence for portraying 16 and 17 June as a serious threat to the existence of the GDR government. Even if one accepts the Western figure of 370,000 participants this constitutes only

6 per cent of the total workforce. Disturbances were reported from only 270 of the nearly 10,000 local administrative districts. Nevertheless these 270 included a number of working-class districts, especially in Leipzig and Magdeburg. Certainly the events came as a shock to the country's political leaders who spent weeks afterwards discussing grievances and complaints with the rank and file. All decisions of 11 June were upheld, and the last doubts about lowering the norms were removed. Most important, the Soviet Union, to aid its struggling German ally, decided not only to wipe off the remaining war reparation payments of US$ 2.537 million but also to grant the GDR massive economic assistance.

The impact of the events of 17 June in Berlin had the further result of undermining the 'heavy industry at any price' policy. Throughout Eastern Europe changes in economic planning resulted. In some countries like Bulgaria, Romania and Albania, where emphasis on heavy industry as against production of consumer goods and agricultural goals had not been so strong, the changes sufficed to ease the tension over subsequent years. Poland was an exception, for here there were clashes between workers and police forces in the western Polish city of Poznan during July 1956.[3] However, it was in Hungary that the situation resulted in an explosion.

The Hungarian government under Matyas Rakosi had the most ambitious plan of all the people's republics to industrialise the country rapidly by emphasising the development of the heavy industrial sector. Whereas the preceding three-year plan (1947-9) had allocated only 25 per cent of the investment fund for industrial development, the five-year plan (1950-4) originally prescribed 42 per cent for industry. As was pointed out earlier, this figure was soon raised. The share of agriculture, which had been 31 per cent in the three-year plan, fell to 16 per cent. The total investment outlay began with 28 billion Forints. After one year this sum was raised to 50 billion and there were further rises throughout the next year until the figure finally reached 84 billion Forints. Hence within two years the target figures for investment trebled. Hungary was to be 'transformed into a country of iron and steel' announced one of the party leaders. This was a rather pretentious claim, as an economic historian has aptly remarked,[4] given the fact that the country had to import 80 per cent of her iron ore and more than 90 per cent of her coking coal.

This unrealistic approach by the Rakosi Government led to severe difficulties which permeated all sectors of the economy. The handicraft trades were worst affected. High taxes and a deliberate policy to cut off most of the supply of materials brought about a decline in the number of gainfully occupied persons in that sector from 273,000 to 42,000 between 1948 and 1952. By the middle of 1953 2,000 villages out of 3,500 were without cartwrights, blacksmiths, shoemakers, barbers and tailors. Zolan Vas, former president of the Planning Office, summarised the situation in October 1952: 'Our present difficulties are in part the bills for the Great Power policy of the "country of iron and steel" ... As a consequence of excessive industrialization and the neglect of agriculture, our national economy has lost its natural balance, which it is now no small task to restore.'

Certainly food supply was hit by a serious agrarian crisis. Party leaders admitted to five main errors. First, the stepped-up pace of collectivisation and the violation of the principle of voluntarism for membership; secondly, the high targets and the frequent changes in compulsory delivery quotas; and thirdly, the use of force in the signing of production contracts. The fourth mistake was the policy of eliminating the kulaks (peasants possessing more than 13 to 14 hectares), while the fifth was the insufficiency of investment for agricultural purposes. As a result of this there was large-scale desertion of the land by Hungarian cultivators. The area left fallow almost tripled at a time when shortages already existed for many agricultural products. By 1952 the standard of living for most of the population had fallen.

As in the other people's republics and in the Soviet Union the shift to the softer 'New Course' which followed the economic crisis of the early 1950s and the death of Josef Stalin, also occurred in Hungary. However the fanaticism with which Rakosi had adhered to the previous course was now matched by an equally ardent pursuance of the New Course. Imre Nagy, who had become the new chairman of the Council, announced in July 1953 a basic revision of the plan. He demanded a better proportioned industrial structure in conformity with the economy's resources, a serious development programme in agriculture, participation of the workers in the internal division of labour and a significant increase in the standard of living. Consequently the whole direction of the five-year plan was changed. Investments were cut in the second half of 1953 and a further reduction was planned for 1954. There were also considerable changes in the allocation of investment funds. Compared to 1953, investment in heavy industry was reduced by 41.1 per cent in 1954 while the share of light industry and food processing was raised by 11.9 per cent and that of agriculture by 20.2 per cent. All factories in the heavy industrial sector were now required to produce consumer goods and the handicraft system was revitalised. The number of gainfully employed persons in the handicraft industry more than doubled between February 1953 and December 1954.

Particular emphasis was laid upon agricultural reform. The principle of voluntary membership of collectives was restored and provision for leaving co-operatives was made. This virtually halved the membership in collectives within a few months. Compulsory delivery quotas were reduced and prices paid for state deliveries were raised. Free lease and tenure of land was now permitted and a more lenient policy towards peasants with large holdings was introduced. All this resulted in a higher standard of living. According to official sources real wages of workers and employees rose by 6 per cent in 1953 and 18 per cent in 1954. However, the overall national income now declined and the rapidity of the reforms caused new economic difficulties. This strengthened the position of those sections in the Hungarian Workers' Party who were opposed to the curtailing of heavy industry and who demanded a stop to the 'right-wing deviationist policies' which were more geared to a 'small peasant economy' than to industrialisation.

The standard Western account of what happened over the next two years is well known. To paraphrase, it states that throughout 1955 and 1956 there was continuous confrontation between Rakosi and his supporters and the Nagy group. In October, Nagy was expelled from the party and Rakosi was reinstated, only to be ousted again in July of 1956 and replaced by Erno Gerö. He too proved incapable of remedying the situation and, in particular, he failed to stem the popular tide demanding the return of Nagy. At the same time the ideas emanating from the Petöfi circle, and especially their arguments for a reformist communism (not unlike that of Yugoslavia), won the sympathies of the workers and other groups in the community. On 23 October students organised a huge demonstration in support of events in Poland, where Gomulka had just been reinstated. This turned into a massive gathering of the populace which continued into the next day. The situation was made worse by the government's decision to call in Soviet troops and the revolt soon spread to the provinces. The desperate decision by the party to save the situation by reappointing Nagy as Prime Minister failed. Nagy tried his best to confine the uprising within limits. However, it is said that the popular will had become so ferocious that nothing short of withdrawal from the Warsaw Pact and multiparty elections were acceptable. To this too Nagy finally consented but before the joy of freedom could finally be realised Russian tanks called in by Kadar eliminated all reformist hopes.

As with all black and white presentations, this account leaves much to be desired. It is true that the ideas circulating in the Petöfi circle aimed at a reform of the socialist system, all of which were introduced in subsequent years. On the other hand, the student demands, above all their call for multiparty Western-style government, lay well outside 're-forming communism'. If the demonstration on 23 October took place in an 'orderly fashion',[5] as one of the major Western writers on post-war Eastern Europe alleges, why did it involve the occupation of radio stations and the removal of national emblems within hours of the initial march? In a social confrontation of the magnitude of the Hungarian uprising it was more than likely that blood would flow. But party officials, members of the military guards and mere by-standers were slain in such an atrocious manner that even some Western observers at the time stated that the scene was reminiscent of the White Terror of 1919 and of the Fascist Arrow Cross.[6] The pictures of the bodies of brutally mutilated victims, a number of which were printed in Western newspapers, undermine the image of the 'noble freedom fighters'. As one enthusiastic Western historian wrote: 'Thousands lay dead in Budapest and in the countryside, but it is no exaggeration to say that the entire nation was delirious with hope and freedom.'[7] How would Western scholars react to such a justification of, say, discontented blacks in Los Angeles or unemployed youngsters in Liverpool slaughtering scores of policemen?

The final decision to pull out of the Warsaw Pact and establish a Western parliamentary system would have meant the end for Marxist-Leninist socialism in Hungary – doubtless a desirable result from the point of view of Western writers. But such an outcome could not be described as reforming a Marxist-Leninist system of government. Nor could such a drastic change in Hungary cause much enthusiasm in the socialist block. It is doubtful too, and contrary to the constant Western claim, that the Hungarian workers – notwithstanding their discontent with Gerö – would have supported a course which would have meant a return to middle-class government. After the situation had eased in Hungary the Kadar Government published a four-part series of documents and information in several languages which questioned the assumption of 'full working-class support' for the uprising. This side of the story is not commented on. Presumably it has been dismissed as an example of fabricated and distorted 'communist propaganda' and therefore of no value. Today, however, the Kadar Government has achieved a position of high national and international prestige and does not give the impression of being ready to resort to publishing falsifications. It is also noteworthy that the Yugoslavs — known for their criticism of the Soviet Union — did, with some qualifications, support the action of the Hungarians. The final claim, that the Soviet intervention put an end to the ever-increasing blood-bath, may well be justified.[8]

In many ways the events of autumn 1956 in Hungary were a turning point in the history of the people's republics. They mark the end of the 'difficult years'. Under difficult conditions, involving considerable sacrifice, the foundation of the new industrialised socialist societies had been laid. The shock of the October events had removed the remaining opposition to easing the extremely rigorous industrialisation drive. Planning became more flexible. The second wave of long-term plans presented more balanced targets with increased investment rates for consumer goods industries and agriculture. The near simultaneous launching of the new plans throughout Eastern Europe was an attempt to co-ordinate the economies of the socialist block more efficiently. In addition, most people's republics continued with their policy of channelling agricultural production into co-operatives, this time paying more than lip-service to the principle of voluntary participation. As will be shown below, in the long run this solved the agricultural problem for most of the countries involved.

Hand in hand with these new economic measures went an overall 'relaxation' of the system, which permeated all spheres of life. Culturally, it was the beginning of the 'thaw', with Poland being the first country to come up with a vigorous new wave throughout the arts. Life and society at large entered a more easy-going atmosphere. Soon, for the first time, Western analysts began to question the validity of the conventional 'Kremlinologist' approach. Attempts were made to view the Eastern European countries as living and developing societies, rather than as a mixture of terror and conspiracy. Sociologists set out to challenge Eastern European 'experts' to abandon the model of 'totalitarianism' which had been wrongly accepted as universal key to the socialist world.[9] Although the 'counter Kremlinologists' had little impact upon the established version, it was a refreshing sign that the countries of Eastern Europe were beginning to be seen as nations with problems and conflicts arising from the dynamics of their social structure. The overall improvement did not, of course, put an end to economic and political difficulties. As industrialisation reached a more advanced stage, serious new economic problems were soon to emerge. Likewise, there soon were to be considerable differences among the Eastern European countries in the international and internal policies they pursued.

Observers are quick to label the forces at work in Eastern Europe.

'Stalinists', 'conservatives' or 'hard-liners' are those who maintain that the international cause of socialism should over-ride national interests and/or who insist on more rigid pursuance of industrial investment at the expense of consumer goods production, and/or those who insist upon the priority of the 'plan' over the 'market' in the market socialism of the 1960s and 1970s. 'Anti-Stalinists', 'progressives' or 'reformers' are those who put the national interest first and/or place more emphasis upon the production of consumer goods. The labels are purely polemical. The founding fathers are rather ambiguous on the topic. Ideally, no conflict can exist between states which are guided in their policies by Marxism-Leninism. Socialism is said to have the great advantage that it enables the national interests of each country to be harmoniously combined with the interests of the world socialist system as a whole. In such a system the patriotism of the people of the socialist countries merges with internationalism. Such an ideal typical situation has never arisen, nor is it very likely to occur in the immediate future. If the history of the first decade of the people's republics was largely monolithic, by the end of the 1950s large-scale differences between the countries of Eastern Europe were becoming apparent.

Notes and References

1. Hans Teller, 'Der kalte Krieg des BRD — Imperialismus gegen die DDR in den Jahren 1952-3', *Jahrbuch für Geschichte*, vol. 16, p. 305.
2. Jonathan Steele, *Socialism with a German Face* (Jonathan Cape, London, 1977), p. 89.
3. See below, Ch. 8, pp. 150-1.
4. Bela A. Belassa, *The Hungarian Experience in Economic Planning* (Yale University Press, New Haven, 1959), p. 32.
5. François Fetjö, *A History of the People's Republics*, (Penguin, Harmondsworth), p. 116.
6. André Stil, *Humanité*, 19 November 1956.
7. Neal V. Buhler, 'The Hungarian Revolution' in Frederick A. C. Helmreich, *Hungary* (Craeger, New York, 1957), p. 352.
8. Note Edward Kardelji, 'Socialism Must Develop' quoted in Jonathan Steele, *Eastern Europe Since Stalin* (David and Charles, London, 1974), pp. 62-72.
9. Note for example, A. Inkeles, 'Models and Issues in the Analysis of Soviet Society', *Survey*, no. 60, July 1966, pp. 3-14; A.C. Meyer, 'The Comparative Study of Communist Political Systems', *Slavic Review*, vol. XXVI, no. 1 (1967), pp. 3-12.

4 THE HUNGARIAN PEOPLE'S REPUBLIC: LIBERAL SOCIALISM?

The immediate aftermath of the events in Hungary during October-November 1956 found the nation in a state of disarray and shock. The losses stemming from the paralysis of production and the destruction of raw materials and goods was estimated to be as high as 22 billion Forint. This economic dislocation was accompanied by considerable public disillusionment with the hapless state of affairs caused by the government's policies. The Hungarian communist movement embarked upon a policy of soul-searching. Accusations were levelled against Rakosi and his supporters, whose policies in the late 1940s and early 1950s were said to have laid the foundation for the October disaster. More serious, however, were the charges laid against Imre Nagy and his group. In early March 1957 an article by Joszef Revai, one of the few ministers of the 'old guard' who had not fallen from grace, was given wide publicity. This former head of the Ministry of Culture urged his readers 'to break immediately and radically with the interpretation of the Central Committee of the Hungarian Workers' Party published in *Szabad Nep* (October 28) which presents the counter-revolution as a national and democratic movement...' Revai alleged that there were still too many concessions to the 'counter-revolutionary myth of the positive role of the Nagy group. It is high time to liquidate this myth.' Finally Revai charged the newly-founded Socialist Workers' Party of Hungary with waging a

> campaign of vague calumnies against Rakosi and Gerö instead of proceeding to a concrete uncovering of the roots of the evil, and Nagy is treated with culpable indulgence. One does not even try to analyze the relations existing between Nagy's policy before and after June 1953 and his open treason of October 1956. Nagy's oppositionist attitude — without being treasonous from the beginning, implicitly contained this treason. Comrades Rakosi and Gerö, whatever errors they have committed, have never betrayed the dictatorship of the proletariat by allying themselves with the counterrevolution.[1]

Although the government of Janos Kadar did not publicly respond to Revai's accusations, the fact that the latter was given such widespread

The Hungarian People's Republic: Liberal Socialism?

publicity made it plain that for the new leadership it was Nagy and not Gerö and Rakosi who had committed the graver crime. The former was finally brought to court on charges of having caused great bloodshed and damage to the Hungarian nation, found guilty in a secret trial by a people's court and sentenced to death and executed in June 1958.

Nevertheless it was the policy of the Kadar Government right from its inception in November 1956 to steer a course clear of both right- and left-wing extremism. It decided to uphold the decision taken in the last days of October. The Hungarian Workers' Party (MAP) was disbanded and the new Hungarian Socialist Workers' Party (SzMP) was founded. To ensure that this new party would not be torn apart by factionalism, the membership was carefully screened. At the beginning of 1957 membership of the Socialist Workers' Party was estimated to be 100,000 as compared to 800,000 for the old Hungarian Communist Party. This number rose to 400,000 a year later and is reported to have reached half a million by the mid-1960s.[2]

Other mass organisations were also reorganised. The unions were given wider powers, a communist youth organisation was established and the Hungarian Democratic Women's Movement, which had been dissolved in October 1956, was reconstituted. To pacify the situation further, the Kadar Government announced wage increases of up to nearly one-third of 1955 incomes. This could not be met from the rise in production of GNP, which increased by only 5 per cent in 1957. Rather it had to be financed with aid from the other CMEA countries. A massive 1.2 billion Ruble loan enabled the government to increase the range of consumer goods so that a basis for economic stabilisation could be laid.

In 1958 the Kadar Government introduced a second three-year plan, which concentrated chiefly on the task of restoring the economic balance. This new plan and the second five-year plan which commenced in 1961 avoided rigid dogmas and unrealistic target figures and instead emphasised a more flexible planning programme in line with existing economic conditions. This showed itself in a more modest rate of accumulation and a better proportioned distribution of investment.[3] The key role of heavy industry was given somewhat lesser emphasis and brought into harmony with available natural resources. Measures were introduced which attempted to base industrial development on increased productivity. Living standards over subsequent years rose by about one third between 1957 and 1960 and consumer goods were given much more importance than in the early 1950s. Television sets, washing machines and refrigerators became readily available and even cars could now be purchased for the first time for private use.

The most drastic changes in the early years of Kadar's Government occurred in the field of agriculture. The role of agriculture in the transition to socialism was given considerable attention in Marxist theory. Both Engels and Lenin had recognised that the millions of small-scale peasants could not just be dispossessed if their support for the revolution was to be secured. On the other hand, small-scale peasant proprietors employing antiquated techniques precluded efficient agricultural production in an industrialised society. Hence developed the idea of forming co-operatives or collectives where the ownership of land and equipment remained with the collective. Before the Second World War Hungary's agricultural production provided for only 70 per cent of the nation's food requirements. By 1958 the distribution of land showed the following pattern: of approximately 1.6 million farming properties, 700,000 were of less than 4 acres, a further 600,000 were between 4 and 8 acres, 250,000 between 8 and 20 acres; 40,000 held properties between 20 and 35 acres and 5,000 were above 35 acres.[4] The collectivisation drive of the late 1950s relied largely upon the carrot rather than the stick. The introduction of a generous insurance system which provided for invalid, health and old age pensions, as well as the fact that proprietors in co-operatives were to earn 10 per cent more per annum than their non-organised competitors, brought about a general willingness to join co-operative farms. Farmers were also able to operate small-scale family private plots as a side line, which added to the growing prosperity of the rural community and made the joining of co-operatives a more attractive proposition. During the winter of 1958-9, 343,000 or 34 per cent of all farmer proprietors, joined the co-operatives. A further 370,000 joined during 1959-60. By 1960 79 per cent of the Hungarian cultivators were organised in co-operatives. The process of reconstructing Hungarian agriculture was virtually completed by 1960, although the increase in agricultural production did not reach the expected level until the second half of the 1960s.

By the early 1960s the Hungarian economy had stabilised, but now new problems began to emerge. Commenting on the new difficulties that had arisen, an Hungarian economist had this to say in the mid-1960s — shortly before the introduction of the new economic model:

> It would be a naive notion to think that the practice of extensive development, of expensive investments with low returns, in production the serious problems of quality, etc. can be overcome in a brief time. It is extremely difficult to dissociate the present state

The Hungarian People's Republic: Liberal Socialism? 57

of Hungarian economy from the economic background created by earlier periods of development, from the system of production structure and planning; it is more difficult to discard burdens of the past, to escape the present consequences of past errors than it is generally supposed to be. It is more difficult to break away from an existing structure and change it than to mark out a good new road without adverse antecedents.[5]

The problems which caused such concern to economic planners in Hungary during the 1960s were common to all socialist countries in that decade, although they occurred at different times depending on the degree of industrialisation. The problems were inherent in the change from 'extensive to intensive growth' which followed the establishment of basic industries.

The concepts of extensive growth and intensive growth were first used by Karl Marx in Volume II of *Kapital*, when he distinguished between extensive and intensive reproduction. In modern socialist economic thought, extensive growth is based on quantitative increases in labour, capital and land, whereas intensive growth relates to increases in overall productivity brought about, for example, by increased efficiency of labour or better utilisation of capital. New processes, labour-saving devices, better factory lay-out, improved quality of products — broadly speaking, technological progress — are the key elements connected with intensive growth. Throughout the 1950s and the early 1960s, the extensive component of economic growth was dominant in all of the people's republics of Eastern Europe. Subsequently, difficulties began to emerge. Waste and stagnation had set in. Labour supply, a major factor in extensive growth, was drying up. The increase of the workforce brought about by the shift from the land to the city, and the progressive introduction of child-care facilities, which gave women the chance to enter the workforce on a large scale, had been fully implemented and the birthrate began to decline. The reclamation of former waste lands had reached a practical limit by the early 1960s and considerable economic losses, largely the result of faulty systems of information, target-setting and incentives, became evident. Economic theorists in Eastern Europe had been aware of these difficulties since the mid-1950s but it was not until the 1960s, when faced with a hefty decline in the growth rate of economic production, that the governments decided to act and introduced a series of reforms. The Polish-Australian economic historian Jozef Wilczynski depicts the following areas of change: a basic liberalisation of planning which now became less prescriptive and detailed, with closer consultation between planners and enterprises. Enterprises were now given greater independence, with the hierarchical structure of economic relationship in part being replaced by horizontal dealings between enterprises. The profit criterion was accepted as the main indicator of enterprise success and the material incentives for labour were strengthened with prices being brought closer into line with production costs (which reduced the need for state subsidies). Moreover, enterprises were given more financial responsibility, whilst production and distribution were more closely linked and, finally, there was a stronger orientation towards foreign trade.[6]

Hungary adopted these new policy guidelines more completely than other Eastern European states. Minor reforms had been introduced in 1963, with some decentralisation of planning and management, in 1964, when capital charges were introduced into industry, and in 1968. After extensive discussion among academics, managers and party leaders the 'New Economic Mechanism' was finally introduced. This new system differed considerably from traditional Soviet planning. Enterprises were now free to decide on the size and range of their products and, within limits, were enabled to enter contractual agreements with foreign suppliers. To stimulate efficiency there was to be greater scope for competition among enterprises. As far as the marketing of consumer goods was concerned, state enterprises were expected to compete with each other, with co-operatives and with the small but significant private sector. Larger enterprises, especially those which held a semi-monopoly position, were to face competition from imported goods.

An even greater deviation from the traditional system of Soviet planning was the change in the role prices were to play.

> 'Prices are seen as having an active role: they should 'balance supply and demand', they should reflect 'value judgements emerging from the market' as well as economic policy. 'Differentiation of profits should influence the shaping of the pattern of production and supply ... and help in bringing about the equilibrium of the market.'[7]

Profitability was to become the key to enterprise activity. Because of the vital importance of foreign trade to Hungary, special attempts were made to link these new policies with the practices of foreign trade. More recently, currency reforms have linked the Hungarian Forint rate more closely to 'hard currency' fluctuations than any other Eastern European valuta. As Alex Nove concludes, this could be described as a

The Hungarian People's Republic: Liberal Socialism?

market socialist manifesto. Its essential features were, above all, the abandonment of obligatory production-plan indicators for enterprises, and of its corollary, administrative supply allocation (no more Gossnab, in other words), with prices, profitability and commercial contract determining what is produced and who buys it. Managers of state enterprises remained responsible to their economic ministries, and could be dismissed by them. Major investments remained the responsibility of the centre, but enterprises could invest in expanding or adapting their output obtaining funds from the state banking system and/or using their own investment funds. This is, of course, essential: there is no point in using profits as a 'stimulant' if the profit-making enterprise cannot obtain the funds necessary to ensure that it produces in accordance with market requirements.[8]

At the same time agriculture was to operate on market lines; farm managements too could decide what to produce and sell and there was a generous provision of incentives. Only essential consumer goods and basic foodstuffs were kept under strict price control.

The new economic mechanisms faced a number of difficulties in subsequent years. Some were caused by internal factors such as 'unfamiliarity with competition' or problems connected with 'income distribution and labour relations',[9] which brought a need for modifications. Others were brought about by external factors, especially by the oil crisis of the early and mid-1970s which had a severe impact upon a nation so short of energy resources. Overall, however, 'a mixture of central planning and quasi-market decentralisation' survived.

How successful was the operation of the New Economic Mechanism? Writing a decade later, and not denying the difficulties which had arisen, an Hungarian economist maintained that the 1968 economic reforms were 'an exceptionally successful undertaking'.[10] Not surprisingly, Western commentators have been more cautious. Nevertheless a West German study of Hungary's fourth five-year plan (1971-5) acknowledged Hungary's performance; national income during these five years rose by 35 per cent per capita, real income was estimated to have risen by 26 per cent for blue-collar workers and by 18 per cent for white-collar workers. By 1975, one third of Hungary's real income was spent on social services. Price rises for basic consumer goods, food items and public services such as transport had risen by 14 per cent over the four years but there was full employment and indeed a shortage of labour. Industrial production rose by 37 per cent. Machine-building, electro-energy production, chemical industries and computer manufacturing headed the growth list. Experts also agree that by the 1970s Hungary's agricultural performance was outstanding. Starting as a food-importing nation before the Second World War, 20 per cent of Hungary's exports was made up of agricultural products by 1971. Even more significant is the fact that these exports account for 50 per cent of total exports to Western (hard currency) nations. Compared to the pre-war years, meat consumption per head doubled. The increase in pork production between 1938 and 1971 was 223 per cent (from 402,000 tons to 900,000 tons). Wheat production also doubled compared to pre-Second World War figures. In 1935 there were 32 million fruit trees in Hungary; this had risen to 100 million in 1971 and the production of vegetables increased by similar margins.[11]

In addition to these economic reforms, much attention has been paid to the position of the workforce. By the mid-1960s a series of far-reaching laws was introduced which altered the electoral system, the role of the Hungarian parliament and the functions of representative institutions of the middle and lower echelons. Part of the reforms of the labour code of 1967 also affected the position of the trade union movement. Leading unionists are now represented on plant management committees and, as in most other socialist countries, the unions are responsible for a number of non-economic activities in the areas of culture, health and social welfare.[12] Today the unions have the right to veto management decisions which violate workers' specific interests. The unions can also institute legal proceedings against workplaces for not observing the labour code or collective agreements.

The position of the worker in society is widely debated in Hungary today, as is shown for example by the foundation of a union-affiliated research institute which is charged, in particular, with undertaking studies on the feasibility of plant democracy. However, although the trade unions' increased sphere of responsibilities and enlarged field of action are ranked as very important, there are difficulties, as is shown by the following comment from an Hungarian sociologist:

> Progress, however, is slower than would be desirable. The reasons are manifold and only partially analysed. Attempts to analyse them are made in many ways, among others by means of empirical studies. One of these studies, carried out in two huge ironworks, pointed out, amongst other issues, the management's reluctant or sceptical attitude towards the usefulness of workers' participation, contrasting sharply with the declared willingness of the workers. (In both plants 50 per cent of the workers declared that the efficiency of the

management could be improved by listening to workers, while in one plant only 15 per cent and in the other 5 per cent of the managers were of this opinion.) Managers gave their reasons in different terms: a substantial percentage voiced the opinion that if the worker is satisfied with his salary, his interest in the plant's affairs stops there. A similarly large group thought participation irrelevant because under the present socialist conditions no management decision could harm the interest of workers. Two smaller groups of managers declared, on the one hand, that workers already had enough say via the trade unions and, on the other, that participation could be enlarged only if the level of technological and general culture of the workers was also raised. It can hardly be doubted that these reasons are ultimately motivated by the managers' present position of power and the interest generated by this position. In other words, the managers are aware that enlarged participation necessarily entails a change in the power structure at their expense. Changing this attitude depends partly on the pressure exerted by the whole of society towards democratization, partly on the emphasis of central party or government organs on democratization. Giving workers more information and more technological and social knowledge is certainly important in making their participation more effective, in improving its usefulness, and in pressing for a change in the outlook and orientation of management.

But again, participation is not a self-sufficient end, although its possible effect on relations within and between groups may be a considerable social gain in itself. Over and above this gain, increased participation has to be directed towards the transformation of the social division of work. This last problem, however, is probably the most difficult of the tasks to be solved.[13]

The position of the unions is only part of the overall debate about future developments and the path towards socialism. The role of the party is given special attention. The party sees itself as the *avant-garde* of Hungarian society, leading it on the road to socialism. The party provides the intellectual and ideological theory and leadership. Party members set the pace in society, take up the leading role. This is not done by force or dictatorship but by a feeling of obligation and responsibility towards the community. Emphasis is on active participation, setting an example and persuasion. According to party rules, 'the communists are committed to develop confidence among the people and the principle of serving the Hungarian nation and the cause of international socialism'.

The liberalisation of the domestic scene was accompanied by the introduction of equally liberal visa laws which have made it possible for the Hungarians to visit the West. In 1963, 120,000 Hungarians were given Western visas. At the same time the events of 1956 were to be forgotten and reconciliation was offered to those Hungarians who had fled the country. This relatively free state of affairs has enabled the Hungarian theoreticians to take the lead in the ideological confrontation with the West about the 'freedom issue', which arose especially at the time of the Helsinki agreements. Through radio and the press, Hungarian commentators have rejected the frequent claim that the socialist countries disregard the Helsinki principles. Their argument is that sections of the Western press are merely rekindling the Cold War.

> It has been a long time since the Western Nations have talked so much and so loudly about freedom as they do at present. We have to go back right to the years of the Cold War to recall a similarly tendentious and heated campaign. But if we compare the propaganda used then with today we note a shift of emphasis. In those days freedom was demanded for the countries of Eastern Europe to liberate them from alleged slavery. But today even the Western countries realize that such arguments are completely ineffective and hence they use more subtle means of propaganda about the topic of freedom. Today emphasis is shifted to individual freedom the alleged absence of which is supported by refering to a few Eastern European dissidents... This method of argument is most popular among the bourgeois propaganda because it diverts attention from the real basis of individual freedom: the right of economic freedom. Who possesses this basic right of freedom, a few or the working masses?... Capitalist society ensures that a few people hold all the means of production as their private property; in socialist society — by sharp contrast — it is the working masses, society which holds the far largest share of the means of production. This fundamental difference is covered up by Western propaganda. If we talk about individual freedom we just simply cannot leave out the right to work, the right to education and advancement. He who is sacked by his factory cannot feel free even if the freedom of speech allows him to complain about having been robbed of his work...[14]

Furthermore, Janos Nagy has written:

> It is not an accident that at a time where the developed capitalist

The Hungarian People's Republic: Liberal Socialism? 63

countries constantly injure the most basic human right, the right to work... a massive campaign has been started against the socialist countries to frighten their citizens with stories about the horror of socialism... The fact that the emigration and immigration laws of the socialist countries are drawn up to harmonize human aspects and individual wishes with the demands of the nation's domestic construction is being presented as a violation of the final accord of the Helsinki agreements. That on the other hand the strict immigration practice of the capitalist countries has not been loosened, that some capitalist countries even ask visa applicants about their position in the party and exclude party members from entry – this is never mentioned... The final accord does not give any nation the right to interfere in the inner affairs of other countries but this is precisely what the organisers of the current campaign do when they demand the strengthening of some 'internal opposition' in the socialist world. Our answer is: We guarantee the real human right, the right to a meaningful human existence, and we reject the attempt to meddle in our affairs...[15]

Nor does the 'dissent issue' cause great enthusiasm among the Hungarian artists and intellectuals. Tibor Dery, a renowned Hungarian writer, gave this reply when asked why he did not sign the Czechoslovakian 'Charta 77':

A messenger was sent to me to ask whether I would sign an address of solidarity by Hungarian Intellectuals with the signatories of the Prague Charter 77. To this messenger – a friend of mine, I said immediately and clearly that for several reasons I would not sign. First there are practical reasons: I see the act of the 34 Hungarian writers who have signed the charter as a gesture of sympathy. This does not lead to practical results or, if it does, it will be in the opposite direction, i.e. it will provide little assistance for Czechoslovakian writers. But [such a step] would harm our writers here in Hungary, our political regime [the regime Kadar] and the minister for culture Pazsgay. As far as the people are concerned there are some well-known signatories among them but in the main they are very young people, who have little experience in matters of politics and in their admiration for the symbol of freedom they may start things without realizing the consequences.[16]

And in an interview with the Vienna newspaper *Die Presse*, the Hungarian

Deputy Prime Minister Gyorgy Aczel had this to say about dissidents: '... there is no history without contradictions. A state without contradictions is possible only in a circle of Angels, who, as we know, do not have a gender nor the ability to change. Creative difference of opinion is a normal state of affairs and a lot of the confused, who are called dissidents are also a normal feature of the human condition.' At a later stage in the interview he alleged that, 'many of the people who call themselves dissidents cannot be taken seriously as they are only after cheap international popularity'.[17]

These comments should not be pushed aside too readily because – judged by any standards – Hungary's cultural output over the last 20 years has been most impressive. The publication of Laszlo Nemeth's novel *The Journey* in 1962 signalled the beginning of a significant literary revival. Although *The Journey* pleads for a compromise between Hungarian nationalism and socialism, it is not without biting comments about current conditions. Notwithstanding this the government regarded it as a positive achievement and it presaged a burst of literary productivity. Reviewing the Hungarian cultural scene three years later, Laszlo M. Tikos, a Western-based observer, was baffled: '... the present-day political climate differs so markedly from that prevailing in the rest of the Communist bloc that one cannot help wondering why this is so'. The reviewer detected three 'surprising factors': first, the degree of freedom allowed to 'the grand old men' of Hungarian literature, secondly, the tolerance displayed towards Western literature, which was now widely available in translation; and thirdly, the fact that topics so far considered taboo were now being dealt with in published writings. This last factor especially provoked the admiration of the critic. Tikos could even state that Hungary now had its own Alexander Solzhenitsyn – Jozsef Lengyel, who had spent a number of years in a Soviet labour camp and was now publishing his memoirs in a series of articles.[18] Tikos was not the only outside observer noticing that 'things were happening in Hungary'. An emigré writer, Paul Ignotus, declared that Hungary held 'Many freedoms, if not freedom itself.' And a Slovak journalist was even more enthusiastic when he exclaimed: 'There freedom bears the name of socialism and Kadar is the most popular man in the country.'[19] This is certainly a change from a few years previously, when the West branded the First Secretary a Hungarian Quisling.

Hungarian films are more accessible to Western observers than literature and film-making in Hungary has not lagged behind the best products of the Western industry during the last two decades. Miklos Jancso's films have been widely acclaimed, particularly *Cantata* (1963),

My Way Home (1964), *The Round Up* (1966), *The Red and the White* (1967), *Silence and Cry* (1968) and finally the erotic epic, *Public Virtue, Private Vice*, which focused on the last days in the life of the Austrian Crown Prince Rudolf before he committed suicide with his mistress – the 17-year-old hermaphrodite, Maria Vetseras – at Meyerling near Vienna. Nor is it true, as repeatedly alleged by Western observers, that 'certain years' in Hungary's post-Second World War history are taboo. Andras Kovacs's film *Stud Farm*, for example, is set in the 'Rakosi years'. The hero, Janos Buso, an uneducated but loyal party member, is appointed manager of a valuable stud farm near the Austrian border; the area is fortified with land mines and heavily armed soldiers patrol the premises. Buso, who knows nothing about horse-breeding, finds that the stud farm is effectively run by officers and non-commissioned officers of the former fascist regime who barely hide their contempt for the new regime. In the superbly photographed Hungarian landscape, the critique of Stalinism unfolds. Buso's brother is called up by security police and taken to a labour camp. There, to his great relief, he finds that he is not to be imprisoned, that instead he is to select from amongst the prisoners a manager for the farm he administers. The prisoners are landowners who have been sent there for collaboration with the fascists. The film shows Rakosi holding court amidst trigger-happy soldiers. In the end, Buso is knifed by the former collaborators, who are then mowed down in their attempt to flee across the border.

The theme of harmonising 'human aspects and individual wishes with the demands of the nations' is taken up in Pal Gabor's film *Angi Vera*. The film is set in 1948. Vera, a naive 18-year-old nurse, publicly criticises the conditions in the hospital where she works. Subsequently she is selected for further political training in a residential school. Here she seduces one of her teachers, Istvan, who (although married) falls deeply in love with her. Vera soon ditches him and in a dramatic confrontation at her graduation he openly confesses his love for her. Vera, who had been honoured as the most successful and industrious student of the course, replies with a public apology: the only thing she regrets was the affair with Istvan because it diverted her from her political duty to master the knowledge of socialism.

The liberalising of Hungary's economy, politics and culture was accompanied by a steady rise in the standard of living. The visitor to Budapest notices that more goods are on offer compared to Prague, even Leipzig and certainly Bucharest or Warsaw. The old saying among socialist leaders that buyers' markets are a luxury because they promote consumption rather than production and that the social costs of channelling resources into non-productive services are high, is not without truth, however. In Hungary, it is housing construction which seems to have slipped down the list of priorities. Housing remains a serious problem throughout the 1970s.

Per capita income for Hungarians in 1976 was US$3,300. This was slightly below the United Kingdom but well ahead of Italy, Greece or Portugal.[20] In the overall standard of living among the CMEA countries, Hungary is ranked second (together with the CSSR) behind the German Democratic Republic and, as far as the range of consumer goods is concerned, Hungary is probably at the head of the socialist countries. The successes of the Kadar Government brought its returns. Even Western observers admit, however reluctantly, that Kadar has the support and respect of the Hungarian people. In an impromptu speech at a luncheon given in his honour on his sixtieth birthday Janos Kadar had this to say:

> My deep conviction is that the humanism of our age consists of Marxism-Leninism as a science, and of communism as an ideology. This means decency, integrity, and humaneness, and its objective is the improvement of human life. At times I say that the relationship between Marxism-Leninism, socialism, and communism on the one hand and the Hungarian working class and the Hungarian people on the other, does not consist of the fact that we possess an excellent theory which we are trying out on ten million guinea pigs. I believe it is the other way round; Marxism-Leninism and the entire communist ideological system exist for the purpose of giving these ten million Hungarians a better life. For if it were not there for this purpose, and something were wrong in this respect, we would not be doing a good job. I am very glad that recognition of this is increasingly gaining ground in our country and people representing Marxism-Leninism are becoming ever more infused by a sense of reality and humaneness, by a regard for and an appreciation of non-communist, and the resulting awareness that we can only progress together . . .[21]

His comment was not an understatement.

Notes and References

1. Quoted in François Fejtö, 'Hungarian Communism' in W.E. Griffith, *Communism in Europe*, vol. 1 (MIT Press, Massachusetts, 1964), p. 227.

The Hungarian People's Republic: Liberal Socialism?

2. Miklos Molnar, *A Short History of the Hungarian Communist Party* (Dawson, Folkestone), p. 48.

3. I.T. Berend, 'Contribution to the History of Hungarian Economic Policies in the Two Decades Following the Second World War', *Acta Historica*, vol. 13 (1967), p. 36.

4. K. Böllinger, *Weltgeschehen*, p. 221; author's conversion of hectares into acres.

5. Berend, *Hungarian Economic Policies*, p. 41.

6. J. Wilczynski, *Socialist Economic Development* (Allen and Unwin, London, 1977), p. 33.

7. Quoted in Alec Nove, *Soviet Economic System*, p. 290.

8. Ibid., p. 291.

9. For detail, ibid., p. 292.

10. Bela Csikos-Nagy, 'The Hungarian Economic Reform after Ten Years', *Soviet Studies*, vol. 30 (1978), pp. 540-6.

11. Gerd Biro, *Osteuropa*, vol. 22 (1972), p. 730.

12. See below, Chapter 5, pp. 73-4.

13. Zsuzsa Ferge, *A Society in the Making, Hungarian Social and Societal Policy 1945-75* (Penguin, Harmondsworth, 1979), pp. 82-3.

14. *Nepszabadsag*, 21.41, p. 3, quoted in *Osteuropa-Archiv*, vol. 27 (1977), pp. 680-1.

15. In *Tarsadalmi Szemle*, 4/1977 quoted in ibid., pp. 682-3.

16. Ibid., p. 683.

17. Ibid., p. 684.

18. 'Hungary: Literary Renaissance', *Problems of Communism*, vol. 27, no. 3 (1963), p. 24.

19. Quoted in Fejtö, *History of the People's Republics* (Penguin, Harmondsworth), p. 169.

20. Note below, p. 143.

21. Quoted in Jonathan Steele, *Eastern Europe since Stalin*, pp. 199-200.

5 THE GERMAN DEMOCRATIC REPUBLIC: ECONOMIC MIRACLE?

For the GDR the 1950s continued to be a decade beset with difficulties. The divided Germany in the heart of Europe became the centre of the West-East confrontation not only in terms of Cold War arguments about reunification and Berlin but also in terms of outright economic competition. Here, in full view of the world, one part of Germany was undergoing reconstruction along capitalist lines while the other followed a socialist course. Not surprisingly it was the GDR government's avowed aim not only to match but indeed surpass the economic performance of West Germany. There was no chance for this to happen quickly.[1] The vastly different starting conditions soon ensured that the Federal Republic surged ahead. This is not to say that the GDR's economic performance was unimpressive. The contrary was true. With relief from the burden of reparations and with the transfer of the Soviet-run joint stock companies in 1953,[2] the GDR economy maintained a steady growth rate. The target figures for the first five-year plan were largely fulfilled and in the wake of the reforms following the July 1953 confrontation, living conditions by 1955 had risen by one third compared to 1950, although there still remained a considerable shortage of consumer goods. The second five-year plan for the years 1956-60 specified an increase in gross national production of 55 per cent. Priority was given to the development of lignite, power and chemical industries. Plan targets were completed by 1958, two years ahead of schedule. The most notable achievement was the construction of the *Kombinat Schwarze Pumpe* which became the world leader in the production of brown coal. Production of consumer goods was also increased and the overall 'surprisingly favourable economic development'[3] led to a further rise in living conditions. But the gap in production between the Federal Republic and the GDR did not decrease; if anything, the former was pulling further ahead. The 'golden lure' provided by the West had a devastating impact upon the GDR economy. Between the foundation of the republic in 1949 and 1960 more than two million people left for West Germany, a fact which greatly undermined the gains the GDR economy was achieving and which provided a constant hindrance to the effective functioning of the nation's economy. The brain drain especially hurt. In 1960 alone 688 doctors, 296 dentists and 2,648 engineers went to the West. As professional people they had been trained at the institutions and at the expense of the GDR, to collect handsome incomes in the Federal Republic, which had, of course, contributed virtually nothing to their education. No country can afford such losses for a sustained period of time, and it is surprising that the government hesitated for so long before finally establishing control over its borders.

The background to the Ulbricht Government's decision to close the border crossings between East and West Berlin and to construct the Berlin Wall was a re-escalation of the intra-German Cold War which reached a new peak in the late 1950s. The GDR government's decision to complete the collectivisation of agriculture led to an increase in the number of GDR citizens leaving for the West. In particular, disgruntled farmers decided to leave. In 1959 144,000 went to the West. This figure increased to 200,000 in 1960, to rise further during the first six months of 1961 to 207,000. This was accompanied by a particularly ferocious anti-GDR campaign on the part of most West German newspapers, which claimed that a 'people's uprising' was imminent. In fact, some newspapers advocated open war:

> The Free World has to reach a position to use all means of cold war, nerve war and conventional war ... this includes not only conventional forces and armaments but also undermining the system by encouraging escalation of internal opposition, underground work, disintegration of all order, sabotage of traffic and economy, disobedience, uprising, revolution.[4]

On 13 August the border was sealed. Western politicians and newspapers expressed their dismay at such action but did not hide their satisfaction that the construction of the Berlin Wall had finally and for all time shown that the West was superior to socialism. The almost hysterical jubilation reached its peak with President John F. Kennedy's visit to the city when he too announced that he was a 'Berliner'. However, in reality many statesmen on both sides were relieved that one of the major world trouble spots was under control. The confrontation between the two German states about the wall has continued to the present day. Yet it laid the basis for a final acceptance of the post-war reality, and consequently for negotiations between Eastern and Western Europe and, later, between the two Germanies. It did not imprison the people of the GDR,[5] as is so often claimed in the West. Rather it finally removed the main source of instability in the GDR and gave the new system a chance to show what it was capable of.

The construction of the Berlin Wall almost coincided with the change in economic direction characteristic of the whole Comecon region in the early 1960s. As in the other people's republics, the economic organisation which emerged during the 1960s and 1970s is based on the principle of 'planning from above to below' which replaced the earlier principle of simply 'planning from above'. The basic principles of economic planning are decided at the top level of the Politburo in co-operation with the other Comecon or CMEA countries, especially the Soviet Union. Legal sanction for the economic plan is provided by the People's Chamber. The highest administrative and planning body is the Council of Ministers and its executive body, the State Planning Commission. The latter, in conjunction with the industrial ministries — of which there are eleven — is responsible for the co-ordination of planning. As such, it submits to the Council of Ministers outlines of structural policy options as well as basic guidelines for annual and five-year plans for the economy as a whole. The State Planning Commission also elaborates the basic plan targets laid down by the Council of Ministers by publishing key information such as tentative guide figures and planning directives. Moreover the Council is responsible for the final co-ordination and dovetailing of draft plans, long-, medium- and short-term planning as well as regional planning. Finally, like the Council of Ministers, it is called upon to arbitrate on specific points of planning and to project balances within the framework of material production.

The GDR economy is based both on the 'production principle' of sectoral direction and the 'territorial principle' of regional direction. Below the Council of Ministers and the State Planning Commission in the sectoral direction are the industrial ministries which are in charge of the plan in their particular field of production. Administration and economic guidance at this level are undertaken through specialist agencies: either the Associations of Publicly-owned Enterprises (*Vereinigung Volkseigener Betriebe*: VVB) or the directly subordinated major combines (*Kombinate*). The VVBs constitute the link between the central economic authorities and the production units (the *Volkseigene Betriebe*: VEB). Within their sphere of competence the VVBs co-ordinate efforts and project balances in the preparation of plans. They are in charge of their VVB fund and thus responsible for promoting and guiding processes of rationalisation in production. They also form the centralised management for research and development.

The combines represent either horizontal or vertical amalgamation of enterprises. Combines are subordinated either directly to the industrial ministry responsible for the particular sector, to a VVB or to an area authority. Combines subordinated directly to the ministries are in charge of functions similar to those of the VVBs such as accountancy and pricing. Horizontal amalgamation predominates in the food-processing and consumer goods industries, in mechanical engineering and plant construction and in the building industry. Vertical amalgamations are mainly found in the metallurgical and petrochemical industries. During the 1970s there has been an increase in the number of combines while at the same time the number of VVBs has declined, although the important role of the VVBs in the GDR economy is not being significantly undermined. According to West German observers, the combines provide the advantage of lower costs through centralisation of such tasks as procurement and marketing; lower investment costs per unit of output achieved by longer production runs at larger plants; and an acceleration of the pace of technological progress through the concentration of resources.

In addition to this 'production principle' of sectoral direction, there is the 'territorial principle' of regional direction. Hence an area-managed sector co-exists with the centrally-directed sector of industry. The area-managed enterprises and combines are controlled by Area Economic Councils, which exercise functions similar to those of the VVBs without however being subject to the principle of commercial accounting. They are responsible to a ministry or an Area Council. Territorial planning concerns the best location of industry, the co-ordination of each enterprise, environmental concerns and settlement planning. Below the Area Council are the District, Municipal and Commune Councils, which all participate in implementing the process of 'planning from above to below'.

The economic reforms of the 1960s connected with the change from extensive to intensive growth set out to rationalise planning methods and avoid petty administrative tutelage. In addition, they aimed to promote greater efficiency by means of the so-called 'economic levers' (*Lenkungsinstrumente*), such as the principle of autonomous raising of funds, production-fund levies, fund-related prices and price dynamisation. This was to be achieved by a carefully balanced system of enterprise autonomy and profit orientation on the one hand and central planning and control on the other. There was also an increased emphasis on the introduction of scientific methods. The VVBs played an important part in what were called the 'New Economic Policies'. Whereas the VVBs were originally introduced as links in the chain from the Council of Ministers to the enterprises, in 1963 their status was upgraded from being purely administrative authorities to being corporate bodies. In a way, the functions discharged by the VVBs under the New Economic System in dealing with their enterprises were comparable to those of the head offices of industrial corporations in the West.

By the later 1960s difficulties had arisen with the 'New Economic Policies'. The new functions of the VVBs had begun to cause setbacks for the central planning mechanisms; the policies of the ministries and the VVBs conflicted and created a degree of confusion; different sets of instructions hindered efficiency and caused over-bureaucratisation. By 1970, serious production setbacks had also occurred and there were particular shortages and strains in the less highly controlled sectors. Thus it was decided to return to a more plan-orientated course. With this return to centralisation the VVBs took up their original functions again as the executive arms of the industrial ministries. Hence the tendency towards a more 'market orientated' economy, which has been noticed in Hungary, was not pursued in the GDR. Instead the GDR concentrated on improving the working of the plan. Most pioneer work in the field of 'structural planning' has been done in the GDR: to quote a Western analyst of socialist economies:

> Under the traditional 'branch' approach, plans are worked out by the relevant economic ministries with the participation of the branch associations and enterprises concerned. Experience has shown that this departmentalization produces sectional pressures for protecting narrow interests, in several ways impeding technological progress.
>
> Under structural planning, the planners' preoccupation is not with individual branches of the economy but with selected broad goals or problems, especially with modernization, specialization, concentration, industrial co-operation, applied research and innovation. Structural plans do not merely consist in an extrapolation of existing situations but in attempts to anticipate the desired structure and direction of development in the future. It is widely realized now that intensive growth critically depends on the continuous assimilation of new technology. To facilitate this process, favourable conditions must be provided for in long-term plans based on economic prognoses to promote the continuity of technical progress.[6]

Although complications and problems continued to arise, as is the case with any economy, after a decade of relatively unimpeded economic growth following the construction of the Berlin Wall, the GDR's industrial achievements were spectacular.

The country was listed among the top ten nations of the world in

The German Democratic Republic: Economic Miracle? 73

terms of gross national product by the end of the 1960s and it had become the economic pace-setter within the CMEA countries. Industrial production per capita clearly surpassed the other socialist countries taking over the leading role of the CSSR.[7]

Agriculture in the GDR also made considerable progress. As in Hungary, collectivisation was completed by 1960. A considerable number of small farmers had joined voluntarily but here too 'strong persuasion' and pressure were used in the end to complete the process. Nevertheless the image of 'forced collectivisation', with its notion of a peasantry maltreated and cowed, is well wide of the mark. However, sizeable numbers of small-scale farmers did go to the West.

The GDR system of rural producer co-operatives consists of three types. In type one, only the arable land is collectively cultivated. All other assets remain in private hands. In type two, cultivation equipment is also operated collectively. In type three, all pastoral land and livestock production are also combined in the co-operative, with provision being made for small-scale private farming and husbandry. These household plots in fact contribute a considerable share of vegetable, egg and fruit supply. The majority of co-operatives are of the type three arrangement. Overall, the co-operatives now account for nearly 90 per cent of agricultural production. This system of producers' co-operatives laid the foundation for a well-functioning agriculture. Large-scale production of agricultural machinery aided the process. By the early 1970s GDR agricultural production had caught up with the Federal Republic and, according to authoritative West German sources, the structure of production offers better prospects for future development.[8] Hence the claim of the GDR government to have mastered the 'agrarian problem' which haunted most of the industrialised countries and still does was no exaggeration.

What does the GDR economic system mean for the rank and file workers? Below the VVBs are the individual enterprises, almost all of which are now *Volkseigene Betriebe* (people-owned enterprises). In charge of the enterprise is the director who is appointed by and responsible either to the VVB or directly to the ministry. His decision-making powers are considerable but there are a number of checks and balances. There are outside controls, like the bank which lends funds and the statutory obligations imposed by the law. But there are also internal checks. The British journalist Jonathan Steele sums it up:

> A factory in the GDR is not only an economic unit. It is also a major element in the country's political and social structure. The main

mass organisations which function in society as a whole operate in the country's factories. These groups – the SED, the production committees, the trade unions, and the social organisations for young people and women – do not exist in order to balance out conflicts of interest. The stated assumption is that there is a complete identity of interest between individuals and the whole society. The factory management, the party groups, and the mass organisations work together as a 'unified, social leadership'.[9]

The SED party branch (*Betriebsparteiorganisation*, BPO) of an enterprise is most influential. The director himself is a member and has to answer to his fellow party members at branch meetings. The BPO forms a link in the chain upwards to the national party apparatus and downwards to the workers' cells. At the same time it also runs the enterprise's newspaper. No doubt, the BPO plays an important role, as do the production committees which are formed of members of the trade unions, the Free German Youth League (FDJ), the Democratic League of Women (DFD) and members of the technical and economic staff. The permanent production committees act as a forum for the management and the various sections of a plant to discuss issues of production.

The trade unions in the GDR differ from their Western counterparts. In the West they are expected to protect the employees' interests versus the employer. In the GDR, to quote Steele:

> They are in charge of all social security funds, from sick pay to the allocation of holiday places in trade union hotels. The trade union is in charge of the factory's hospitals and clinics. Under the collective contract the factory is committed to spend money on *creches*, kindergartens, new sports facilities, leisure centres and housing. The trade union supervises industrial safety, and ensures that the factory management observes the rules. On this the GDR's record is particularly good.

The West German government's 'Report on the State of the Nation' in 1971 admitted that industrial accidents hit 8.8 per cent of the workforce in the Federal Republic but only 4.1 per cent in the GDR.[10] The trade unions also keep watch over the system of workers' training and further education.

A great deal of argument over the last two decades has concentrated on the role of centralised planning in the socialist economies. Some Western observers praise 'encouraging tendencies' towards a more liberal, competitive market economy, which is alleged to have reached its fullest development with the CSSR reform model. On the other hand, various strands of 'worker control' ideas permeate 'new-left' or 'third way' writings. The fact that the GDR has strongly adhered to a centrally-planned economy is commonly explained as the result of political 'hard-line' expediency. The truth of the matter is more complex: there has been extensive debate in the GDR about reformist or revisionist economic theories. These have usually been rejected because to GDR theoreticians they are a distortion of Lenin's principle of economic centralism. Participation of the workforce in planning and running enterprises is based on the theory of uniting two factors: the achievement by means of socialist democracy of increased production efficiency in the nation's economy and the fostering of collectivist attitudes and improved educational standards throughout society. The socialist concept thus maintains that the individual can only achieve his or her optimum development by learning to master the material process of production. The inclusion of an ever-larger circle of the workforce in planning aims to eliminate alienation from the means of production which stems from the preceding capitalist eras; until eventually the stage is reached where the social differences between non-manual and manual labour are overcome. This goal, however, cannot be achieved without central management and control. Hence the integration of the individual unit into the overall working of the plan is essential. Large-scale decentralisation in the functioning of the enterprises can never achieve optimum returns for society as a whole. Decentralisation of individual enterprises would undermine the basis of democratic centralism because, without central co-ordination, enterprises would once again reach the stage of competing with each other. The common interest of the working people would be replaced again by rival and opposing interests.

> Without the planning and management of the whole economy, without the leading role of the party of the working class, a policy of individual enterprise autonomy would ignore society's overall interest and hence be ineffective. The most important force for development, the coordination of personal and collective interests within the demands of society as a whole, would be lost. This would inevitably mean enterprises being set against each other. The consequence of this would be — as the revisionists demand — the emergence of competitive market conditions. This however would involve abandoning the ultimate goal of our policies, namely the development of the

socialist individual within the socialist community. In its place then would appear once again the social Darwinist principle of the fight of all against all.[11]

Participation of the staff in all matters of running the enterprise can only be successful if the enterprise is integrated in the nation's overall plan. Between units there should be competition but not destructive competition. Socialist competition is the prerequisite for the fulfilment of plan goals. The principle of market competition which seeks market and profit advantages is firmly rejected by GDR ideology. The reintroduction of such policies would lead to the establishment of a competitive socialism which would eventually create a monopoly position for individual enterprises at the expense of the workforce. It would in fact hand over the economic power to the local industry managers without reintroducing private ownership of the means of production.

How can increased participation of the workforce in the decision-making process of 'democratic centralism' be achieved? The current state of development of socialist society still requires the principle of director management. However, it is the task of the director not only to run the enterprise efficiently and productively but also to educate his staff into recognising their democratic function. Indeed it is the duty of the director 'besides fulfilling the necessary technological and economic functions to undertake every effort to ... prepare the basis for an active participation of the workforce in the management ... In all spheres of labour the duty in part of the persons in charge is to educate. Only when a person in charge has fulfilled this duty can the task be said to have been consummated.'[12] The key role education plays in preparing the individual for participation in the running of his work place is recognised by law.

On a more practical level, the staff participates in the formation of the plan through their various organisations such as unions, and youth and women's leagues. They may participate either directly in staff assemblies or by sending delegates to plan discussions. The most important of these committees are the production committees, which have considerable say in the drawing up of the plan. It is the committee's duty to analyse and comment on the plan before the latter is passed on to a higher body such as the VVB. The production committee is also expected to keep a check on the directors and, in cases of serious disagreement, the committee is entitled to seek arbitration from the general director of the VVB. Only experienced and well-qualified staff members are normally on production committees.

Thus, to summarise, it is obvious from this that the Marxist interpretation of the term 'democratic' is based on a vastly different principle than the Western interpretation. The abstract Western notion of political democracy has little relevance for the socialist means of production. Democratic socialism aims to enable the workforce to participate as owners of the means of production in all collective decisions. The decisive basis for this process has been created. Socialism does not require the establishing of a countervailing power to limit that of the employer, such as the union in the capitalist world. The socialist means of production demand something quite different: collective guidance and planning of the production process on the basis of society's ownership of the means of production.[13] This is of course a slow process requiring a high level of education amongst the workforce. But the many discussions about increasing the role of the workforce in planning shows the importance that government and planners attach to this task.

Theoretical discussions notwithstanding, the economic achievements of the GDR have had more immediate results concerning the everyday life of the people. The standard of living has risen steadily over the last 20 years and today only in the richest Western nations does it surpass that of the GDR. By the mid-1970s per capita national income exceeded such relatively affluent Western countries as the United Kingdom and New Zealand. Per capita national income in itself is no indicator of living standards and the strength of the GDR lies in its outstanding social welfare, health and education policies. As early as 1965, a Unesco study ranked the GDR's child-care facilities such as creches and kindergartens as the best in the world. Since then they have been even further improved. By the mid-1970s there were 403 creche places for every 1,000 children. The availability of kindergarten places for three-, four- and five-year-olds was more than 800 per 1,000 which meant that virtually every family was able to find a kindergarten place for its child. Today mothers receive a grant of 1,000 marks on the birth of each child and they are entitled to take a year off work on full pay. This programme, however, is not intended to promote marriage and childbearing. Jonathan Steele came across this answer given to an 18-year-old girl in the advice column of the youth newspaper *Junge Welt*. The young girl had asked whether she could 'drop out':

> We expect more today from an 18-year-old girl than taking refuge in having babies and being 'married comfortably' with a husband who makes enough money. Personal and social thoughtlessness coincide here ... If a girl of your age, and your stage of training and economic

dependence wants to have a baby with all her might then this shows that she has either been seduced by a family idyll which no longer accords with the social atmosphere, or she has simply not thought things out enough. Your husband's salary may provide a guarantee for your marriage and your personal life, but as you know money alone does not make people happy, and even less so if you earn not a penny of it yourself. Training and a job are not only a means to obtain financial security but also foster the equality of wife and husband, mutual recognition and respect and the intellectual atmosphere of a marriage. The best way to prepare for your baby and your marriage is to take a clear decision on your future. You should discuss this with your parents, your fiancé, and your teachers. But you can only expect understanding and help from them if you make proposals that show you do not simply want to lead a comfortable life.[14]

Education too plays a key in the GDR. In this field, by the mid-1970s, the West German magazine *Der Spiegel* conceded that the GDR had surpassed the Federal Republic:

In proportion to the population the GDR has 70 per cent more teachers than the Federal Republic. Eighty-five per cent of the pupils complete a tenth year at the general polytechnic school, the GDR's standard type (which is still a long-range target in the FRG). Ninety-nine per cent of all GDR school-leavers learn a profession or trade; in the Federal Republic 10 per cent stay without training. The GDR invests more than 7 per cent of its GNP in education, a sum which is only a target for the 1980s in the FRG (today it is 5 per cent). Out of every thousand people between 18 and 45, seventeen were attending a polytechnical college or university compared with fourteen in West Germany. Student numbers in the GDR jumped from 280,000 in 1965 to 390,000 in 1972. People already in jobs can go on learning. About 168,000 GDR citizens are taking correspondence courses at training colleges or universities or are in evening classes. The statistics of success also make clear the increasing equality of women. In 1972 more than half the students at technical colleges were women, and at universities more than a third. In the Federal Republic only about 25 per cent of the students are women.[15]

All health, medical and hospital services are comprehensive and free and the GDR government also encourages an extensive 'preventive health' programme. There is ample provision for sport and recreation both indoor and outdoor and the citizens are urged to participate in one of the many sporting competitions. The spectacular GDR international sports successes of the last two decades were only made possible by massive provision of sporting facilities at the 'base level'.[16]

Living costs have remained low, and virtually static for many years, which means a net gain as wages have continued to rise. Housing costs are low compared with the West and on average amount to not more than 5 per cent of a person's income. The housing sector had been severely neglected until 1970 which created a serious problem. With the appointment of Erich Honecker to the position of First Secretary of the SED in 1972, however, housing construction was given first priority. Between 1970 and 1980 more than 1.3 million flats were built and a further 300,000 were renovated. The planners hope to have overcome the housing problem by 1990.

The stability provided by these policies soon produced results. By the end of the 1960s, Western analysts estimated that the new system had won the loyalty of almost three-quarters of the population.[17] This position further improved during the 1970s.[18] Western observers who approach the topic 'GDR' with intentions other than merely to malign the country have also commented upon the comparatively cordial relationship between state and Church. The exemplary way the GDR incorporated its only ethnic minority, the small group of Lusatian Serbs, into the state, has also been noted.

The situation as far as consumer durables and luxury goods are concerned is not so favourable. Black and white televisions, radios and washing machines are in abundant supply, although prices for these items are much higher than in the West and colour televisions and modern hi-fi equipment are difficult to obtain. Cars too are more expensive than in the West. There is a waiting list of eight years for a car, or four years for a married couple, and the current ratio of cars to population is still considerably lower than in Western countries. Today one in three families possesses a car and, if the current trend continues, by the end of the 1980s the ratio of cars to population should have reached Western proportions — presumably with similar traffic problems. Luxury goods are now available in hard currency shops although this is a source of some ill-feeling, as not everyone has access to Western currency. Certainly production of consumer durables is still a weakness of the economy, although the gap with the West is narrowing. An obstacle to the achievement of exceptionally high levels of production of consumer durables is the questioning as to whether the crass materialism of the West is a desirable objective, especially in view of the appalling levels of poverty in the Third World.

The satirical magazine *Eulenspiegel* and the cabaret *Die Distel* provide vehicles for the criticism of mistakes and shortcomings in the nation's everyday life. The *Distel* cabaret, with its sharp wit, is especially popular and is always booked out for many weeks in advance. Criticisms, complaints and suggestions for improvements are not left to the satirists alone but are encouraged in everyday life and at the work place. This leads to the question of how to explain the confrontation between the government and various writers in recent years and beyond this to the 'Wall' and the visa policies which no doubt constitute the country's Achilles heel. The conventional Western claim which attributes these solely to the machinations of the East German 'Stalinist hard-liners' sadly distorts the complexity of the issue. Ever since the end of the Second World War the country has been at the centre of the East-West confrontation. It was – and in part still is – the 'German problem' which stood in the middle of the Cold War. It may have eased at times but it has never been solved. Up to the late 1960s the Federal Republic's Hallstein doctrine aimed at eliminating the other German state. It was the achievement of the Brandt Government to attempt and in part to achieve normalisation of relations between the two Germanies in the early 1970s. For this the former West German Chancellor was deservedly awarded the Nobel peace prize. But his policy was approved by only a small majority of the German population and there are still strong forces in the FGR who refuse to accept the post-war reality. The powerful Springer press for example, which pursues a never-ending crusade against the other Germany, still prints the term GDR in inverted commas. It is not so much the economic loss which hurts when a person defects to the West but the propaganda which such a step gives rise to. The person is invariably celebrated as a national hero who has risked his or her life in order to gain political freedom in the West. That most people head westwards for material gain is not mentioned. And a Western analyst would have to research very widely to find out that in 1977 for example, in addition to the 4.3 million pensioners, 41,000 young people were given permission to go West.[19] The publicity concentrates upon the people who leave without visas. In a spectacular incident in 1979, a couple of families with children managed to cross into the Federal Republic by balloon. Although many people on both sides were dismayed that the parents subjected their children to such a highly dangerous act, the escape was hailed as a further example of the lengths to which people were prepared to go to get out of the country.

Most Western press empires outside Germany joined the jubilation and at times the newspaper coverage reached the absurd.

Early in 1980 the Ballet of the Berlin Komische Opera toured Australia. The company, almost 100 people strong, performed in most of the Australian capitals and, notwithstanding a busy schedule, the young people had ample opportunity to move around the continent. Press speculation about the inevitable escapee accompanied the company's performances through the tour. Nothing however happened until on the very last day when a young ballerina failed to turn up for the departure. The dancer made it clear from the very start that she was not staying behind for political reasons. She had fallen in love with a Melbourne restaurant proprietor whom she later married. Nevertheless the Australian government insisted on granting her political asylum (the last time an Australian government took such a step was in 1954). The Australian press went overboard on the topic. A press conference with the 'political refugee' was transmitted live and nationwide and the Australian newspaper publisher Kerry Packer offered $35,000 for her life story. This sort of incident is both offensive to the GDR and an illustration of the inane lengths to which the Western capitalist media can go. It is against this sort of background that the fortress mentality of the GDR has to be seen. They are in the midst of the ideological confrontation and indeed bear the brunt of the attack. This explains the sensitivity about the open criticism by some of their leading writers – criticism can be made without playing into the hands of the country's opponents. This also explains the government's unwillingness to introduce more liberal visa laws for travel to the West, such as those that operate in Hungary, Poland and the CSSR. Recent years have shown that there are ways to negotiate and arrive at mutual agreements. The people who would benefit from such a mutual agreement would be precisely those people for whose well-being the Western press claim to be the spokesmen.

Notes and References

1. For a recent publication on the GDR note Jonathan Steele, *Socialism with a German Face* (Jonathan Cape, London, 1977).
2. Joint stock companies were set up after the war when 200 enterprises in the Soviet occupation zone were formed into companies effectively under Soviet ownership to produce for the Soviet Union.
3. *Handbook of the Economy of the German Democratic Republic*, German Institute for Economic Research (Saxon House, Farnborough, 1979), p. 7.

4. *Kölnische Rundschau*, 10 July 1961.
5. See below, p. 80.
6. Jozef Wilczynski, *The Economics of Socialism* (Allen and Unwin, London, 1970), pp. 65-6.
7. For details, ibid., *passim*.
8. Hans Immler, 'Hat die DDR die Bundesrepbulik schon überholt' in Konrad Merkel and Hans Immler, *DDR Landwirtschaft in der Diskussion* (Verlag Wissenschaft und Politik, Köln, 1972), pp. 43-70.
9. Steele, *Socialism with a German Face*, pp. 129-30.
10. Ibid., p. 132.
11. J. Arnold Ritterhaus, 'Zu einigen Problemen der sozialistischen Demokratie in Industriebetrieben-Gedanken zur soziologischen Analyse dieser Problematik' in *Wirtschaftswissenschaft*, vol. 3 (1969), pp. 373-83, quoted in Willy Wyniger, *Demokratie und Plan in der DDR* (Paul Rugenstein Verlag, Köln, 1971), p. 128.
12. Autorenkollektiv, *Arbeitsrecht der DDR* (Berlin, 1968), pp. 71-4, quoted in Wyniger, p. 124.
13. The demand by various left-wing theoreticians for the maintenance of the autonomy of the unions is not reconcilable with the concept of democratic socialism. There is no employer against whom the workforce has to protect its interest.
14. *Junge Welt*, p. 179.
15. Ibid., p. 171.
16. Note the author's 'Politics Only' in *Sport in the GDR*, McKernan and Cashman (eds.), *Sport in History* (University of Queensland Press, 1979), pp. 86-98.
17. Hans Apel, 'Bericht über das Staatsgefühl der DDR-Bevölkerung', *Frankfurter Hefte*, vol. XXII, no. 3 (March 1967), p. 171.
18. See below, Chapter 10.
19. Hartmut Zimmermann, 'The GDR in the 1970s', *Problems of Communism*, vol. 27, 2, 1978, p. 36.

6 ROMANIA: MEDIATOR BETWEEN EAST AND WEST?

After the consolidation of power by the Communist Party the early history of the Romanian People's Republic followed a comparatively quiet course. As in the other people's republics, priority was given to rapid industrialisation but the pace of progress both in the introduction of heavy industry and in the modernisation of agriculture was more modest than that of Romania's socialist neighbours. It was not until 1958 and especially after the commencement of the six-year plan (1960-5) that the development of heavy industry accelerated. The modernisation of agriculture by the formation of co-operatives was completed later than in the other people's republics.[1] Notwithstanding this slow beginning, however, the circumstances of Romania's economic 'take-off' in the late 1950s and early 1960s created a huge controversy in the CMEA countries which forms the background to the spectacular foreign policy course initiated by Romania.

The background to the growing economic crisis of the CMEA countries is well known.[2] During its first years of operation, the role of the CMEA was confined to the registration of bilateral commercial agreements between its members. By the mid-1950s, however, the member states began to work towards a degree of specialisation, drawing up a list of key materials in order to harmonise supply and demand for those materials throughout the socialist world. The first signs of conflict between the more developed countries (GDR and Czechoslovakia) and the less developed countries (Albania, Romania and Bulgaria), with Poland and Hungary somewhere in the middle, became visible at the May 1956 CMEA meeting which discussed specialisation in the area of machine tools. The Czech delegation in particular expressed concern about what they saw as the narrow outlook of some of the economic officials. Writing on the Romanian economy, Montias summarised the situation.

> There were also some officials from the more developed countries, including Czechoslovakia, who did not sufficiently understand the necessity of transferring the production of certain machinery products to the less developed countries, especially products requiring a less complicated technology. There, already, was the crux of the problem. Items such as tractors, trucks, roller bearings, lathes, and

combines, which generate significant economies of scale when produced in large quantities, present relatively simple technological problems; they can be taken over profitably by the underdeveloped countries, leaving the less profitable large-scale manufacture of complex equipment for the metallurgical, mining, chemical, and paper-making industries to their more advanced partners. The unwillingness of the industrialized nations to yield standardized, apparently highly profitable, manufacturing activities to the less developed countries was one of the prime causes of the friction in CMEA.[3]

That it was especially the Czech economists initially who urged the formation of a supra-national trading community became evident in subsequent years when a number of theoretical treatises were published which denounced 'autarchic tendencies' and instead advocated 'international specialisation'. Although the developed socialist countries seemed to gain most from the pooling of the region's economic resources, the case for a supra-national trading community was not without a certain logic. At a time when their resources were strained to achieve a sound economic basis from which to compete on the international market and consolidate their domestic position it did seem reasonable to co-ordinate their resources to the benefit of everyone. On the other hand this would mean that the pace of industrialisation in the 'underdeveloped' countries of Eastern Europe would slow down considerably and simultaneously their overall dependence on their developed neighbours would greatly increase. Not surprisingly this caused some resentment in the industrially less advanced socialist countries and it was Romania which soon emerged to spearhead the attack upon economic integration.

A Western journalist once described the Romanian First Secretary, Head of Party and Prime Minister, Gheorgiou Dej, as a 'man of limited intelligence but a remarkably cold blooded and astute tactician'.[4] Nevertheless, to judge from the way Dej handled the CMEA crisis of the late 1950s and early 1960s, one must credit him with intelligence as well as astuteness. The Romanians did not take long to respond to the Czech demands for more integration by stating their own position of defending their protectionist policies. The debate with the Czechoslovaks and the East Germans – and also, from about 1961, with economic theoreticians from the Soviet Union – continued over the next three years with both sides adopting an increasingly firm stand. The issue was further aggravated by the Romanian decision to open up stronger trade links with the West and, by February 1963, at a meeting of vice-premiers of member states in Moscow, the confrontation reached its first peak. At this meeting the representatives from the Soviet Union, the CSSR and the German Democratic Republic made a last-ditch effort to reorganise CMEA into a supra-national agency that would be capable of initiating and supervising the execution of specialisation agreements. The split that resulted from this conference was so serious that Dej called a special meeting of the Romanian Party Central Committee which congratulated the delegates for having upheld Romania's stand at the conference. The bickering continued for several months without achieving any progress towards reconciliation. By now Dej had taken the issue to the public in a widely publicised debate which culminated in the publication of the 'Statement on the Stand of The Romanian Workers' Party Concerning the Problems of the World Communist and Working-class Movement' by the Central Committee of the Romanian Workers' Party in April 1964-5. Here are extracts from key passages:

> Cooperation within CMEA is achieved on the basis of the principles of fully equal rights, of observance of national sovereignty and interests, of mutual advantage and comradely assistance.
>
> As concerns the method of economic cooperation, the socialist countries that are members of the CMEA have established that the main means of achieving the international socialist division of labour, the main form of cooperation among their national economies, is to coordinate plans on the basis of bilateral and multilateral agreements.
>
> During the development of the relations of cooperation among the socialist countries that are members of the CMEA, forms and measures have been projected, such as a joint plan and a single planning body for all member countries, interstate technical-productive branch unions, enterprises jointly owned by several countries, interstate economic complexes, etc.
>
> Our party has very clearly expressed its point of view, declaring that, since the essence of the projected measures lies in shifting some functions of economic management from the competence of the respective state to that of superstate bodies or organisms, these measures are not in keeping with the principles that underlie the relations among the socialist countries.
>
> The idea of a single planning body for all CMEA countries has the most serious economic and political implications. The planned management of the national economy is one of the fundamental,

essential, and inalienable attributes of the sovereignty of the socialist state — the state plan being the chief means through which the socialist state achieves its political and socioeconomic objectives, establishes the directions and rates of development of the national economy, its fundamental proportions, the accumulations, the measures for raising the people's living standard and cultural level. The sovereignty of the socialist state requires that it effectively and fully avail itself of the means for the practical implementation of these attributions, holding in its hands all the levers of managing economic and social life. Transmitting such levers to the competence of superstate or extrastate bodies would turn sovereignty into a meaningless notion.

All these are also fully valid as concerns interstate technical-productive branch unions as well as enterprises commonly owned by two or several states. The state plan is one and indivisible; no parts or sections can be separated from it in order to be transferred outside the state. The management of the national economy as a whole is not possible if the questions of managing some branches or enterprises are taken away from the competence of the party and government of the respective country and transferred to extrastate bodies.

This document signalled the failure of a supra-national CMEA. The debate continued for some time before it was eventually scaled down. Obviously neither side was interested in bringing the issue to a real head. The CMEA organisation remained intact, in future differences were to be worked out more smoothly. Dej had won, Romania was to continue with its rapid industrialisation and with its policy of increasing trade links with the West. Dej died one year after this achievement and his successor, Nicolae Ceaucescu, was to shift the emphasis in Romania's new course from economic to international relations.

The man who succeeded Gheorgiou Dej was relatively young, 47 years of age on his election as First Secretary. With his elevation, a number of younger members entered prominent positions and Ceaucescu from the start left no doubt that he would continue, and also expand upon, his predecessor's policies. He set out immediately on a practical and theoretical level to revitalise a 'Romanian nationalism'. He introduced a series of measures which resuscitated the concept of Romanian socialism. In this he followed Gheorgiou Dej's first careful steps[6] but he added so much vigour that an excited Western observer declared in 1965, merely one year after Ceaucescu had taken office: 'By the end of 1964 the

Romanian leaders were bursting with self-confidence and obviously enjoying the success of their economic policies at home and abroad.'[7] This was accompanied by theoretical propositions about the concept of national communism. Romanian theorists maintained that the concept of the nation state, far from becoming obsolete, was still an essential basis for communism. For a long time to come the nation would be 'the form of human community which is historically necessary'.[8] To support their argument they claimed that history had demonstrated that a socialist revolution springs out of the contradiction within a nation and it succeeds because it is headed by the people of that nation. Moreover, as each nation is culturally and economically distinct with special traditions and problems, socialist decision-making must take into consideration these national peculiarities. Consequently socialist inter-state relations are based on 'the principle of national independence and sovereignty, equal rights, mutual advantage, comradely assistance, non-interference in internal affairs, observance of territorial integrity'.[9] This, of course, is not to say that national communism can function without international communism. To quote Ceaucescu:

> There is no national communism and international communism; communism is national and international at the same time ... By building socialism, every people fulfills a national task and at the same time an international one, contributing to the general advance of mankind toward socialism.[10]

As this suggests, the guiding principles of proletarian internationalism must be:

> ... strict observance of the principle that all Marxist-Leninist parties enjoy equal rights, of the principle of non-interference in other parties' domestic affairs, of each party's exclusive right to solve its own political and organizational problems of appointing its leaders [and] orienting its members in problems of internal and international politics.[11]

In essence this is no different from the stand taken by the other socialist countries. But such a theory gives no real indication of what should be the over-riding principle — in case of an emergency such as the Czechoslovak crisis of 1968[12] — namely, international socialist solidarity or national independence. It also leaves open the question of the degree of emphasis with which Romania, unlike the GDR for example, has always stressed the national element.

The approach of the Romanians led from the mid-1960s to a foreign policy which diverged considerably from the rest of the CMEA countries. Even before Ceaucescu's rise to office Romania had drawn world attention to its foreign policies when, in January 1963, Romania was the first, and so far the only country in Eastern Europe — other than Yugoslavia — to re-establish diplomatic relations with Albania.[13] One year later Romania made history by adopting a position of neutrality in the steadily deteriorating Sino-Soviet dispute. But the real blow fell after Ceaucescu had become First Secretary. The diplomatic recognition of the Federal Republic of Germany as part of Romania's drive to improve trade relations with the West caused concern among most of the country's neighbours and outright dismay in the German Democratic Republic and Poland. Both their reactions are understandable. The GDR after more than a decade of the West German Hallstein doctrine was finally making some headway in establishing her recognition in the world outside the socialist camp. Under the Hallstein doctrine the Federal Republic threatened to break diplomatic ties and cut off economic aid to any nation which questioned the Federal Republic's claim to be the only legitimate German state, by recognising diplomatically the existence of the GDR, or the Federal Republic's claim to the territories east of the Oder-Neisse frontier. In the struggle with the Federal Republic they had greatly appreciated the solidarity of the other socialist countries and Romania's defection came as a serious blow. Hence the GDR's discomfort was not altogether unfounded and the Romanians' reply to complaints from the GDR was rather lofty: 'Is the author of the article [in *Neues Deutschland*] perhaps unaware that the foreign policy of a socialist state is laid down by the party and the government of the country in question and that they have to account only to their people and nation?'[14]

The Poles' protest rested on the West German government's refusal to accept the Oder-Neisse line, the post Second World War boundary between Poland and the GDR. A large part of the modern Poland was east of the Oder-Neisse. The Romanian step was the more ill-conceived — from an Eastern point of view — as the aim of achieving favourable trade relations was not fulfilled. However, the heat was taken out of the issue sooner than expected when it became clear that the establishment of diplomatic relations between Romania and the Federal Republic of Germany was only the first sign of a dramatic change in West German foreign policies under Willy Brandt. In the following years Brandt, first as Foreign Minister then as Chancellor, successfully pursued a policy of recognising the post-war reality, which was one of the major factors aiding the development of detente in the early and mid-1970s.

In 1967 the Romanians undermined the solidarity among socialist countries by siding with Israel over the Israel-Arab conflict and in 1968 Ceaucescu condemned the occupation of Czechoslovakia by Warsaw Pact troops in no uncertain terms as:

> ... a flagrant transgression of the national independence and sovereignty of the Czechoslovak Republic: interference by force in the affairs of the Czechoslovak people; an act in complete contradiction with the fundamental norms that must govern relations between socialist countries and Communist parties, and with the generally recognized principles of international law.[15]

However, after consultation with the Warsaw Pact allies, Ceaucescu ceased to attack the invasion. There was one last piece of showmanship in the 1960s when in 1969 the US President Nixon was given a huge welcome in Bucharest. But with the new decade in its foreign policy, Romania shifted from the 'spectacular' to the more productive role of 'honest broker'. She now acted as mediator on a whole range of issues: between the Soviet Union and the Eastern European states on the one hand and China on the other, between Israel and the Soviet Union, between the industrialised world and the poorer countries and especially in the move towards detente between East and West. Romania's claim to have played a vital part in the staging of the mid-1970s Helsinki meetings is not an exaggerated one.

On the domestic scene Romanian policies were not nearly as colourful. The economic reforms — especially the tendency towards decentralisation — which were characteristic of the region throughout the 1960s were, of all the socialist nations, the least pronounced in Romania. This is not altogether surprising because, notwithstanding the drive towards industrialisation during the last years of Gheorgiou Dej, by the mid-1960s, as Table 6.1 illustrates,[16] industrialisation was the least developed in Romania of all the Eastern European CMEA countries.

As Table 6.1 shows, in 1950, the proportion of the population of Romania employed in agriculture was roughly equal to that of Bulgaria and Yugoslavia and not far behind Hungary and Poland. Yet by 1967 Romania was the only country where the proportion of its population employed in agriculture still exceeded 50 per cent. This explains why the centralist economic policies pursued by the Ceaucescu Government resembled more the style of the 1950s and the same can be said about

Table 6.1: Percentage Distribution of Working Population According to the Main Branches of the Economy, 1950, 1960 and 1967

Country	Year	Industry[a]	Construction	Agriculture[b]	Transport[c]	Others[d]
Bulgaria	1950	11	4	73	2	10
	1960	22	5	55	4	14
	1967	28	7	43	2	20
Czechoslovakia	1950	30	6	39	5	20
	1960	37	8	20	6	29
	1967	39	8	18	7	28
GDR	1950	39	6	23	7	25
	1960	42	6	16	7	29
	1967	42	6	15	7	30
Hungary	1950	20	3	51	4	22
	1960	28	6	38	6	22
	1967	33	7	29	6	25
Poland	1950	19	4	57	4	16
	1960	22	6	47	5	20
	1967	24	6	42	5	23
Romania	1950	12	2	74	1	11
	1960	15	5	65	3	12
	1967	20	7	54	4	15
USSR	1950	22	4	46	7	21
	1960	25	6	39	7	23
	1967	29	7	30	8	26
Yugoslavia[e]	1953	8	3	67	2	20
	1961	14	4	57	3	22
	1967	19	5	48	4	24

(a) includes manufacturing, mining, quarrying and crude processing of primary products.
(b) including forestry.
(c) including communications.
(d) includes trade, other productive branches and the non-productive sphere.
(e) Data for the whole economy (as distinct from the socialised sector) are available only for census years (1953, 1961). Figures for 1967 are J. Wilczynski's estimates.

his policies towards the state and party. The economic growth rate after 1965 was certainly spectacular: about 10 per cent during the last years of the 1960s to 11 per cent in the 1970s. Still the gap between Romania and the other CMEA countries narrowed only slowly. The percentage of people employed in agriculture had fallen to 47 per cent by 1972. As Ceaucescu admitted at the second state conference, Romania was still a developing country. Annual income at that time was in US$ 500-600 or well below that of the more advanced socialist countries, not to mention affluent Western countries. This situation did improve in subsequent years but again only modestly. By the mid-1970s, living standards and per capita income in Romania were still at the bottom end of the table of CMEA countries. At that time voices began to be heard questioning the wisdom of the Western-orientated policies. It was pointed out that the role of 'honest broker' had ensured that on the one hand the CMEA countries were not greatly inclined to place Romania at the top of their list for aid and on the other hand the Western nations were not quite as generous in their economic hand-outs as they were with their praise of Romania's independent foreign policies. Not surprisingly, in recent years Romania's independent stance has been less evident than it was in the late 1960s. There are still occasional incidents when Romania 'snubs Moscow', not all of which are productive. In 1978 Romania refused to join an international flood-control scheme in which the other Eastern Danube countries participated. As a result parts of Hungary were flooded, with heavy losses to that nation's agricultural production. A year later thousands of Hungarian and other tourists from other Eastern European countries were caught by Ceaucescu's sudden decision to sell petrol to visitors for Western currency only. The step was taken with no prior notice and greatly inconvenienced many Eastern European visitors. As this shows, Ceaucescu these days seems to be satisfied with minor issues. Western observers at party congresses might note a particularly long ovation for the Chinese delegation or the absence of 'ceremonial', which is said to be characteristic of the party congresses of 'socialist parties in the brother-countries'. On the other hand, even Western observers admit a strong tendency towards a personality cult which stands quite in contrast to the situation in Hungary, for example.

Romania's cultural scene also has received little praise over the last decade and a half since Ceaucescu took up office. It is claimed by one writer, Ian Coja, that Romania has upheld the strictest censorship laws of all the socialist republics.[17] This, however, may change with the officially announced relaxation of censorship in 1977. The treatment of the Hungarian minority in Romania has also led to a number of complaints by the former and it seems that the allegations by the Hungarians have not been unjustified.[18]

These incidents notwithstanding, the Romanian foreign policies of the last two decades have been a significant factor in Eastern Europe and in Europe at large. Claims which denounce Romania's independent course as window-dressing for Soviet policies[19] merit as little credence as the statement often made in the West that 'freedom in foreign affairs was brought by restrictive domestic policies'. (In the same vein, apparently, domestic policies were permitted by the Kremlin because of Kadar's obedient stance on foreign policy.) As with all countries, Romania's internal policies are linked to and influenced by the international power situation. But in the case of both Hungary and Romania, their policies have stemmed primarily from their own domestic considerations.

The previous chapters have shown that among the people's republics in terms of economic, domestic and foreign policy there is far more 'room to move' than is often credited by Western observers. This obviously leads to the question of how the occupation of Czechoslovakia in 1968 could occur. We turn to this question in the next chapter.

Notes and References

1. On the background see J.M. Montias, *Economic Development in Communist Rumania* (MIT Press, 1967).
2. Ibid., pp. 187 ff.
3. Ibid., p. 191.
4. Fejtö, *History of the People's Republics*, p. 21.
5. Quoted in J. Steele, *Eastern Europe Since Stalin*, pp. 125-7; also, Montias, *Economic Development*, pp. 217-18.
6. David Floyd, *Rumania: Russia's dissident ally* (Pall Mall, London, 1965).
7. Ibid., p. XII.
8. Robert L. Farlow, 'Romanian Foreign Policy: A Case of Partial Alignment', *Problems of Communism*, vol. 20, no. 4 (1971), p. 56.
9. Ibid.
10. Quoted in ibid., p. 57.
11. Ibid.
12. See below, pp. 110-12.
13. Albania had left the CMEA group in the time of de-Stalinisation.
14. In Fischer-Galati, Stephen, *The Socialist Republic of Rumania* (Johns Hopkins, Baltimore, 1969), p. 78.
15. Quoted in J.F. Brown, 'Rumania Today, the Strategy of Defiance', *Problems of Communism*, vol. 18, no. 2 (1969), p. 35.
16. From J. Wilczynski, *Socialist Economic Development and Reform* (Macmillan, London, 1972), p. 190.
17. Quoted in *Osteuropa-Archiv*, vol. 29 (1979), pp. A254-6.
18. *Osteuropa-Archiv*, vol. 27 (1977), pp. A751 ff.
19. Vladimir Socor, 'The Limits of National Independence in the Soviet Bloc: Rumania's Foreign Policy Reconsidered', *Orbis*, vol. 20, no. 3 (1976), pp. 701-32.

7 CZECHOSLOVAKIA 1968: A REAPPRAISAL

For the first two decades after the war Czechoslovakia, as the country was called until it renamed itself the Czech and Slovakian Socialist Republic in 1960, had probably the smoothest passage of the Eastern European nations. The abandonment of the country by its Western allies at Munich in 1938, and the harsh treatment meted out to the Czech and Slovak people by the Germans and their fascist allies, encouraged the emergence of a pro-Soviet feeling which was not confined to the industrial proletariat but also extended to the rural population and even sections of the middle class. The Soviet-Czechoslovakian friendship treaty of December 1943[1] was welcomed by most of the nation and, with the exception of the Stalinist trials during the early 1950s, few shadows fell over the relationship between Czechoslovakia and the Soviet Union or the other European socialist countries. With minor exceptions the political and economic history of the country remained stable for almost a generation. One such exception was the shock to the Western-orientated section of the Czechoslovakian upper and middle class of the events of February 1948 and the resignation of non-socialist members of the government. However these groups, whilst a significant minority, were nevertheless a minority.

The new president from 1948, Klement Gottwald, who died in 1953, was succeeded by Antonin Novotny who also remained First Secretary of the Communist Party of Czechoslovakia (CPCz) and President until January 1968. Novotny has invariably been described in all Western accounts as 'conservative', Neo-Stalinist, 'opportunist' and/or 'unscrupulous' and was severely criticised for opposing, or at least not supporting, the 'writers' revolt' of the mid-1960s and, later, with trying to curb attempts to change the course of the Communist Party. One may readily concede that compared to the doggedness of the GDR leader Walther Ulbricht or the ability to manoeuvre and compromise of Janos Kadar, Novotny did not really succeed in finding a path between the firmness of the former and the flexibility of the latter. Whether this was because of Novotny's personality or because of the surrounding circumstances does not really concern this study. Suffice it to say that the overall balance sheet of the Czech and Slovakian Socialist Republic as 1968 approached was not unfavourable. Industrial growth throughout the 1950s took a steady course. The General Index of Industrial

Production trebled between 1948 and 1958. Table 7.1 sets out growth figures for selected industries and items.[2]

Table 7.1: Growth Figures for Selected Industries and Items in Czechoslovakia 1948-58

Industries and items	1948	1958
Electricity (billion kwh)	7.5	19.6
Manufactured gas (billion m3)	0.6	3.6
Hard coal, net output (million tons)	17.7	25.8
Brown coal, net output (million tons)	22.6	54.3
Pig iron (million tons)	1.6	3.8
Crude steel (")	2.3	5.2
Diesel engines (thousand hp)	110	818
Tractors (thousand units)	9.1	24.6
Passenger cars (thousand units)	18.0	34.6
Domestic refrigerators (thousand units)	8	66
Domestic electric washing machines	2	80
Wheat flour (thousand tons)	589	935
Meat products	77	173

The housing sector was badly neglected during the 1950s but construction was increased in the 1960s. Real wages rose by about one third during the 1950s. Overall national income was estimated to have risen from 100-219 per cent between 1948 and 1958 and real wages were estimated to have risen from 100-123 per cent.[3]

The Czechoslovak communist leaders were also in the comparatively privileged position of introducing farming co-operatives with the backing of the rural population. Collectivisation was gradually introduced between 1950 and 1961. According to a West German agriculturalist, 'the new agrarian policy was intelligently adapted to the traditions and the natural conditions in the country'.[4] Initially, four types of co-operatives were introduced. In type one, the members simply pooled their arable land for joint cultivation. Machines were used partly on an individual, partly on a co-operative basis. In type two, the land passed into co-operative ownership; boundaries were ignored during tillage work. Crops were harvested co-operatively while animal production continued on an individual basis. The proceeds of the joint harvest were distributed largely according to the land brought into the co-operative by each member. In type three, the arable farming and animal husbandry were collectively organised. A household plot with a few animals was left to each member to be farmed as an individual holding. The proceeds were distributed partly according to work done, partly according to the land contributed. Members were paid both in cash and in kind. Production in type four was similar to type three but remuneration was no longer dependent on the land contributed by each member on joining.[5]

The number of type one and type two co-operatives gradually disappeared over subsequent years. The introduction of social insurance systems greatly improved the position of the rural population who were also given access to improved vocational opportunities, social advancement, regular working hours, holidays and a secure income. During the 1968 reform period there were no attempts by the farming community to undo the system of rural organisation, although they did ask for some modifications.

By the late 1950s, and especially by the early 1960s, difficulties had arisen, the nature of which has been extensively commented upon above (see pp. 56-8). As the CSSR was industrially among the most advanced of the CMEA countries it was here that the pinch was felt first. The active role played by Czech economists in the discussion about a transnational CMEA organisation[6] is in part explained by the need to solve the problems that had arisen.

Writing in the post-1968 period, a Western economic observer dealt with the economic crisis of the early 1960s. Not surprisingly, he arrived at the conclusion that 'the depth of the recession and the slowness of the recovery can be explained primarily by the operation of the Soviet system of central planning and management and Soviet development strategy in Czechoslovak conditions'.[7] From this, Professor Bernasek deduces that the recession and dislocation of economic life caused by the limitations of the Soviet model led, by the early 1960s, to a policy which rejected dogmatism in economic theory and revived critical and creative economic analysis. The rejection of Soviet dogmatism encouraged the reintroduction of the market mechanism and rational economic prices:

The recession undermined the authority of the party leadership and brought about open criticism from writers and intellectuals culminating at the IV Congress of the Czechoslovak Union of Writers in June 1967. Finally, it resulted in the removal of A. Novotny and the process of liberalization which was taking place in Czechoslovakia until August 1968.[8]

Here then in a nutshell is one — very popular — interpretation of the wider causes of the 'Prague Spring': economic mismanagement created by the Soviet system. However, that phenomenon cannot be explained so simply. In a reply to Bernasek's argument, Josef C. Brada expressed some strong objections.

> While it is pleasant to attribute calamities to elements which we dislike, such connections are not always valid. That Czechoslovakia had a recession is obvious; that it was a result of the Soviet system of management is not. Indeed, upon close examination it appears that the major difficulties occurred not because of the Soviet model of central planning but rather because of Czech tinkering with it. Furthermore, once the Czechs had recentralized the system, only a series of exogenous events prevented the economy from resuming the rapid rates of growth which the Soviet model had been able to generate in the previous decade, and, incidentally, also during 1965 and 1966.[9]

Brada points to the fact that after extensive discussion and criticism the third five-year plan, which began in 1958, saw the introduction of changes to the economic planning mechanisms. The main emphasis was upon decentralisation of investment in manufacturing and construction. Enterprises were given permission to make use of a number of devices to achieve high rates of profits which led to a huge increase in investment.[10] And although Brada points out that socialist economies can sustain investment expenditure of such magnitude for a long period of time if properly controlled and co-ordinated, the Czechoslovakian economy was neither controlled nor co-ordinated. Brada gives an example from the automobile industry where automobile plants increased their output without a corresponding increase being made by firms producing tyres and glass. Such chaotic conditions were obviously not conducive to sound economic management and the authorities decided to recentralise the economy in 1961. This recentralisation reversed the negative trend, but the planned rates of growth were not achieved in

1962-3. However, Brada does not attribute this shortcoming to the central planners or the system of management but to 'exogenous events'. The low figures were caused by a drastic fall of 18 per cent in agricultural production. If agricultural output had remained at the 1961 level, national income would have grown at a rate of 3.5 per cent. The fall in agricultural production was brought about by the extremely harsh climatic conditions of the 1962-3 winter, which lowered the availability of export goods, at a time when foreign exchange was used for the import of extra coal. 1964 was another poor year in agriculture which prevented a more rapid recovery. But by 1965, the economy was back to previous growth rates and national income by 1966 had grown by over 10 per cent.[11] Hence it is incorrect to speak about a massive economic problem for Czechoslovakia before 1968.

The situation in the CSSR during the latter part of the 1960s resembled in many ways that of Hungary, the GDR or the Soviet Union with economists, economic theoreticians, plant managements, government ministers and representatives from various other institutions working on plans to achieve a more dynamic economic performance. None of the informed writers on the 1968 crisis seriously maintains that the pressure for reform, which was demanded first by sections of the intelligentsia and later by communist representatives in the National Assembly, was based upon a 'broad swell of popular discontent'. Rather, the new policies and the reasons behind them had to be explained to the people. (Of course it would also be difficult to argue that the policies of the Novotny Government were accepted with great enthusiasm.) The situation in the CSSR before the great storm is probably best described as placid and uneventful at least as far as the bulk of the population was concerned. For the writers, intellectuals and intelligentsia it was a different story.

The liberal revival, the 'great thaw' which had swept Poland, Hungary — and, indeed, even the German Democratic Republic — flourished in the Czech and Slovak lands too.[12] The Kafka conference of 1964 was the first outstanding event at which many critical voices were heard and, above all, the Writers' Congress of 1967, with its massive attacks upon Novotny, is often seen as the real starting point for the events of 1968. At the same time attempts were made to rehabilitate the victims of the Stalinist trials and to compensate their relatives. A series of new measures was also introduced. In 1963 Commissions of People's Control were set up to represent the interests of society as a whole against narrow party sectarianisms. In the same year four Central Committee commissions were set up to look into the role of the Central Committee

(CC), to deepen collective leadership and to assure participation of all CC members in the consideration of key issues and in the formulation of party programmes. Election procedures for the National Assembly provided a wider choice of candidates and moves were made to 'deepen the activity' of the National Assembly and the Slovak National Council. These steps were aimed at 'democratisation' but they were hastily dismissed by Western writers as sham reforms. However, the fact that there were no reprisals against the Kafka conference of 1964 or the Writers' Congress of 1967 does not support the conventional argument that Novotny's Government was 'reactionary' and 'neo-Stalinist'.

The first problem the scholar observes in the treatment of the 'Prague Spring' of 1968 is the incredible subjectivity of the terminology used. Invariably Western commentators and Czech and Slovak emigré writers refer to those people who backed the reformist cause as 'progressive', 'enlightened', 'forward-looking'; their arguments are 'devastating', 'precise', 'sharp' and 'convincing'. Their opponents are labelled conservatives, ultra-conservatives, reactionary, Stalinist or neo-Stalinist. Eastern European vocabulary ranges from 'right-wing communist', or 'right-wing deviationist' to the more serious 'counter-revolutionaries'. The opponents are classed as 'left-wing communist', 'genuine socialist' and 'reliable long-standing members', etc. Many writers are aware of the subjectivity of their approach. However, being convinced of the righteousness of their views, they see this as an asset rather than a hindrance. This chapter, however, will refer only to 'supporters' and 'opponents' of the new course.

The chronology of the events seems to be relatively uncontested. The XIII Party Congress held in May/June 1966 had decided to authorise an enquiry into the 'position and leading role of the Party in the Present Stage of Development of our Socialist Society'. The famous Fourth Writers' Congress of 1967 intensified the debate and, by the end of that year, the pressure on Novotny to resign mounted because he was seen as the main obstacle to reforms. There were fiery confrontations in the Central Committee during its October and December sessions until finally amidst further violent clashes Novotny was replaced as First Secretary by Alexander Dubcek. Only three years previously, the latter had been considered by a Western 'Kremlinologist' to be a 'staunch party apparatchik'.[13] Over the subsequent eight months Dubcek set out to steer the CSSR on a course of what was called 'socialism with a human face'. Dubcek throughout this period attempted to steer a middle course between the two opposing sides, although the supporters of reform had a majority in the National Assembly. During the next months the debate spread from the parliamentarians, writers and intellectuals to the party branches, newspapers and other media and also, gradually, to other sections of the public. An initial climax was reached with the publication of the action programme in April 1968 by the Czech Communist Party. Jonathan Steele aptly sums up the programme:

> The programme gave assurances that freedom of assembly would be implemented 'this year' and that censorship would be eliminated. Victims of the purges would be rehabilitated more quickly, and more exact and precise guarantees would protect the right to hold minority opinions. The constitution would guarantee the right to travel, and Czechoslovak citizens would even have the right to live abroad for extended periods. The programme promised to limit the activity of the security police simply to matters involving state security.
> Its central section dealt with the deformations of democracy in the past and the role of the party in the future. The party had to earn its respect. It could not impose it. As for reconciling different interest groups, this job was given to the revived National Front, which was supposed to become a forum for genuinely thrashing out political differences.[14]

Now there was no holding back, widespread debate took place over the entire political spectrum. New political parties were founded. The rehabilitation of the victims of the Slansky trials was speeded up, plans for more satisfactory arrangements between the Czech and Slovak nationalities were passed and soon implemented. Supporters of reforms urged the government speedily to introduce the action programme before their opponents could stop it. Elections were held for a new 'National Front' which was to formulate and introduce the new Czechoslovak model. But before this assembly could meet, troops from the Soviet Union, the GDR, Poland, Hungary and Bulgaria occupied the country. Whereas there have been some differences about the nature of the Hungarian uprising of 1956 there has been no such deviation about Czechoslovakia in 1968. With the former event, not all writers supported 'the people's battle for freedom'. For example, the GDR dissident Rudolf Bahro in his acclaimed book *The Alternative in Eastern Europe* has no hesitation in dismissing the Hungarian uprising of 1956 as a counter-revolution. Prague 1968, on the other hand, was to Bahro not only the 'glorious revolution' of the intelligentsia but also a real chance for socialist progress. Only once in the 60 years since the Russian October Revolution have the forces pressing for a new organisation of non-capitalist industrial society fully appeared in the light of history. Certainly, the moment was a short one, but they were at least able to develop positively to the extent that their real features, their real possibilities and perspectives, could be approximately assessed. This moment was those first eight months of 1968 in Czechoslovakia, which are so unforgettable for all those in the East European countries who are committed to socialist progress.[15] To Bahro obviously, Czechoslovakia 1968 was the chance to perfect socialism. To the Czech emigré sociologist Vladmir V. Kusin, it was essentially a Czechoslovakian kind of socialism, stemming from Czechoslovakia's national background and its socialist tradition. The concept of the new 'National Front' was not unlike the Yugoslav model, but in essence it was Czechoslovakia's unique attempt to 'humanise' socialism.

The 'pluralist' interpretation of the events in Prague is very popular among Western writers. The decision to allow one or more independent parties to operate alongside the Communist Party was a first step towards 'genuine pluralism'. (Genuine pluralism is a roundabout way of advocating Western-style party government on the lines of a neutralist liberal-bourgeois, social democratic state such as Austria and Finland.) This course, it is recognised, would not have been possible under Dubcek. But to some this would have been the eventual – and desired – outcome, so the pallette of interpretations of what was aimed at ranges from reform of the existing system along the lines of the Yugoslavian model to the liberal-bourgeois democracies of Austria and Finland.

Given this variety of interpretations can we really discover what the aims of the reform movement were? The economic proposals were essentially the work of Ota Sik, economic theoretician and for a short period Minister for Economics in the Dubcek Government and later Professor of International Economic Relations at Basle University, Switzerland. When advocating changes in 1965, Sik wrote:

> As the building of socialism progressed, the standard of living rose considerably, workers' real wages rising in 1963 to 164 per cent of the prewar level. The industrial potential of socialist Czechoslovakia substantially exceeded that of the prewar bourgeois republic, which already then ranked among the industrially developed countries.
>
> But the comparatively rapid rate of growth notwithstanding, the emphasis on extensive rather than intensive development resulted in a lag in efficiency. It was necessary to expand production facilities, to build new capacities and enlarge the old, and to bring more manpower into industry. But for all that the exhaustion of the extensive

sources of output growth made it imperative to turn to intensive development for the sources of greater efficiency which the existing system of planning and management had failed to reveal. By the sixties the economy, together with the continued lag in efficiency, began to lose its dynamic quality. It became obvious that the existing system of management could not ensure the necessary radical and lasting upswing in the economy.

There are times, in particular the transition from capitalist to socialist economy, when strict centralised management is necessary. Centralisation helped us to accelerate the social and structural remoulding of the economy and to ensure progress along socialist lines at a time when the class composition of the managerial personnel underwent a radical change and it facilitated rapid equalisation of the economic levels in the various parts of the country. But as socialist economic development gradually got into its stride, rigid centralised planning and management became the main impediments to greater efficiency . . .[16]

By February 1968 his wording had become far more forceful:

Ota Sik emerged as a sharp critic of the 'half-way' and 'inconsistent' implementation of economic reform and a persistent advocate of more decisive action. In many speeches, articles, and interviews, he waged a campaign against unnamed 'demagogues' and 'conservatives' who were throwing the blame for economic difficulties on the reform and were incorrectly predicting that its full introduction would have harmful effects on wages and employment. Prior to January, Sik argued, the political climate and the constellation of forces in the leading organs had blocked the application of the reform principles and had created an atmosphere of fear which discouraged frank discussion. Conservative forces were still seeking to hinder reform and to conserve old practices. He assigned the cause for economic difficulties and inadequacies to the administrative system of management and on the failure to replace it consistently and quickly with a new economic system.[17]

Ota Sik nevertheless did not reach his most radical position from a reformist point of view until after the 1968 period when as Professor for International Economic Relations he formulated a 'third way' between Eastern planning and the current state of capitalism. These ideas, however, were more suited to the 'third way' and 'convergence theories' which were popular topics in Western academic circles in the early 1970s than to the reality of the Czech economy in 1968. The steps discussed and planned in the CSSR did not measure up to the Hungarian New Model which was discussed and introduced during the same years, about which much less fuss has been made but which was by and large successfully put into practice. One wonders, therefore, if one can really talk of the 'symbolic incantation' of Ota Sik.[18]

Nor would anyone argue that the literary revival, the liberal intellectual breeze, was confined to Czechoslovakia. It is interesting that the Hungarian or Polish *literati*, who did not shrink from strong criticism, adopted on the whole a far more constructive approach than their Czech colleagues. From the documentary evidence presented in Western accounts, the majority of the Czech writings were bluntly negative. For example, to argue that the experience of individual alienation which constituted the main theme of Franz Kafka's writings can be experienced in a socialist world — as it can be in a capitalist one — is a reasonable enough assertion. But to present Kafka as a commentator on the Stalinist period[19] seems far-fetched. Thus at a time when their colleagues in Hungary (a nation no less honoured by a long and proud history of indigenous culture than the Czech lands) were criticising injustices and wrongs but simultaneously trying to mould their cultural past with the present, the Czech writers merely put forward a vague and lofty concept of a new cultural Jerusalem. To quote one of their speakers:

> The entire story of this nation, evolving from democracy, Fascist subjugation, Stalinism and socialism (amplified by its unique ethnic problem), includes all the essential features which make the 20th century what it is... In this century this nation has experienced probably more than many other nations and, assuming that its genius has remained alive, it probably knows more. This greater knowledge might transform itself into an emancipating transgression of existing boundaries...[20]

The Czech writers certainly did not suffer from a sense of modesty. Another speaker at the Fourth Writers' Congress had this to say:

> I do not think that Czechoslovak socialism can bring the world now or in the immediate future any important contribution, supported by practical proof, in the field of economy. But in the field of culture and cultural policy it is in the position of doing so.[21]

Such goals allowed for little compromise and there was obviously no other approach towards Novotny and his government than that of condemnation. Perhaps the confrontation between Novotny and the *literati* occurred because the former, unlike Janos Kadar, was not capable of striking a balance with enlightened intellectualism. Or possibly, the confrontation occurred (as one of the writers suggests) because the Czech intelligentsia felt alienated on account of receiving neither material nor moral recognition. On the other hand, the claim by a noted Czech academic, that Czech scholarship tends to suffer from eclecticism and 'excessive abstract thinking'[22] may explain why the Czech intelligentsia failed to adapt to a more pragmatic approach.

There was a great deal of theorising about the relationship of the party to the nation and the people and about the creation of an elected representative institution which was more in harmony with the composition of the population. Zdenek Mlynar, who was probably the chief theoretician behind the later 'action programme' and the constitutional development in general, did not regard a Western multiparty system as a viable possibility in a socialist country. He suggested a 'pluralist National Front'. Kusin summarised his argument thus:

> This National Front, comprising political parties and public organizations, was to become the platform for the 'shaping of overall policies, which would then be elaborated by the state institutions into the policy of the state'. The monopoly of decision-making vested in the Communist Party would be abrogated and handed over to a pluralistic National Front. As an opposition platform – outside the National Front – would not be tolerated, the move would in fact entail the widening of the monopoly to the point where only a very small part of the population would remain without influence on political decisions. Would the National Front monopoly still be a monopoly? The trade unions, numbering some three million members, were one of the National Front organizations. Practically every citizen was a member of one of the organizations of the National Front.
>
> The National Front would form a government which would always be a coalition government. Both the majority and the minority would be represented in accordance with election results. (What Mlynar had in mind were genuinely free elections with a choice of candidates submitted by the member organizations of the National Front.) He suggested that this might be an optimal arrangement for socialism. The principle of the National Front, conceived in this way, also had the advantage of recognizing as political other organizations besides

the political parties. As it was necessary to allow the expression of the widest possible range of diverse group interests, this system might be even better than simple multiparty pluralism. Political parties are always dominated by a small group of people, which is the weak spot even of traditional liberal parliamentary democracy.[23]

The leading role of the party was not challenged — it is after all *the* pillar of Marxism-Leninism — but to prevent further curbs on the possible misuse of power Mlynar suggested measures to ensure a reliable division of legislative, executive and judicial powers, the independence of state and public organs in relation to the Communist Party and direct access of public organisations to such bodies as unions and the youth and women's movements.

By the end of 1967 the demand for changes left the stage of discussion and entered the realm of practice. The leading institutions of the Communist Party initiated the first changes. As stated above, the Thirteenth Party Congress had ordered an enquiry into the role of the Communist Party and when a 'Thesis' was released in Autumn 1967 it soon caused a crisis at the top of the hierarchy. The confrontation began at the October Plenum when Dubcek launched a strong attack upon the Thesis as it neglected to deal with the question of individuals holding more than one office. (Novotny was both First Secretary and President.) This confrontation continued on a more acrimonious level at the December Plenum. There Ota Sik delivered a stronger attack upon Novotny's position and that of other party leaders and after weeks of further heated debate Novotny was replaced as First Secretary by Dubcek on 5 January 1968. Both sides now went to the rank and file to muster further support for their cause and Novotny certainly still enjoyed considerable support in the factories. Nevertheless he was ousted from the position of president when he was replaced on 21 March by General Ludvik Svoboda. By this time the media had joined in with many arguments both for and against the new steps. A first climax was reached in April with the action programme. This programme was a sound document for change, a cautious combination of adapted parliamentary democracy with elements of direct democracy under enlightened communist supervision. It stayed within the boundaries of Eastern European socialism. In fact it received a favourable reception by the Soviet *Pravda* newspaper.

Over the next months the first steps of the programme were implemented. Dubcek attempted a steady but gradual approach as far as the programme was concerned, which was realistic in view of the fact that there was still considerable opposition to it throughout the Communist Party and among the 'masses'. The working population in particular remained critical, even hostile, to the programme throughout the reform period.[24] However, the almost fanatical zeal of the writers was now also becoming evident amongst some of the politicians. The pro-reform section proceeded with firm determination to attempt to build their Rome in one day. As sociologists and revolutionary theoreticians assure us, the time for extremely rapid social, political and economic changes is restricted to 'revolutionary situations' such as existed in parts of Europe this century after the two world wars. At relatively stable times, even if there is a series of problems, attempts at changes and reform are more successful when undertaken at a slower pace, as many Western Labour and Social Democratic Parties have found out over recent decades. Most Western observers realised that the reformers acted so precipitately and justified their action by referring to the necessity to act quickly before the opposition could thwart the whole undertaking. But if this fear really did prevail, it would have been all the more reason to proceed carefully by persuasion to win over as many as possible. However, this is not a correct claim. Although the arguments were hectic, the opposition supported the majority decision when it came to the vote. The old party discipline of showing unanimity after discussion seemed to have prevailed.

The constant rush and pressure made Dubcek's 'centrist' approach very difficult and at times one wonders whether he was in fact still in command. Whilst the politicians tried to make the programme work, intellectuals, writers and journalists had a field day. New parties arose and both sides staged huge meetings to demonstrate public support. Theories covering the full field of the political left and beyond were expounded and with it went a fair share of anti-Sovietism. Ivan Svitak, allegedly a Marxist philosopher, claimed that the Czechoslovak system remained a 'totalitarian dictatorship'. In a speech, 'With Head Against the Wall', he set forth a detailed analysis of the nature of this 'totalitarian dictatorship', which he termed 'our enemy number one', and appealed for a movement 'from a totalitarian dictatorship to an open society'. 'We want democracy, not democratization. Democratization is a minimal program on the way to democracy.' The aim must be to eliminate the monopoly of power by means of elections — free, secret and democratic — 'with a competition of alternative programs and personalities'. Svitak proposed the building of at least two new parties, on a Christian and socialist basis, which would provide 'a healthy opposition to the communist program'.[25]

Although the Dubcek Government repeatedly stressed that the new course was not aimed at ending the nation's friendship with the Soviet Union or their socialist neighbours, the publication of a statement called 'The Two Thousand Words' made these claims less convincing. The 'Two Thousand Words' statement was a blunt condemnation of the last 20 years of history and of the Communist Party. The latter was accredited with only one positive achievement, namely to have initiated the current wave of reform.[26] It could hardly be described as a document propagating constructive changes and if, as Gordon Skilling alleged, it was published to alert the public to the threat to the democratisation movement, it could scarcely have been clumsier. Although all leaders strongly disassociated themselves from the 'Two Thousand Words', the statement caused alarm in the other socialist countries. Hitherto their reaction had been calm. The GDR and Poland were irritated about the CSSR *rapprochement* with West Germany but the action programme had received a favourable press. Now this policy changed. The Soviet Union, GDR and the other states wrote a letter of concern and warned that, notwithstanding the right of each brother nation to pursue its own course towards socialism, they would not be willing to accept such a blow to the cause of international socialism as the transition of the CSSR into a neutral country. This led to the meeting between the Czech leaders and the signatories of this 'Warsaw letter' at Cierna and Bratislava about which little is known. A joint communiqué announced that an understanding had been reached and the danger of further confrontation seemed to have been removed.

The constant reiteration by politicians and others that the Czechs and Slovaks were 'attempting "socialism with a human face"' did not aid the situation because it was as arrogant as it was ill conceived. Both Hungary and Poland had by 1968 a fairly well-established liberal tradition, especially in the arts, and these countries were also working on improving the relationship of the party with the rest of the nation. And countries which at that time did not pursue such a policy, like the GDR, failed to do so not because their leaders preferred to be 'inhuman' to their citizens but because they faced a series of problems which were not present in the CSSR. One can also discern that notwithstanding the talk about 'democracy and humanism' there was an element of 'und willst Du nicht mein Bruder sein, so schlag ich dir den Schädel ein' (if you don't want to be my brother I will smash your skull in). A group of workers who signed a letter addressed 'to our Soviet friends', thanking them for the concern shown about the new political course, brought some very hostile reactions. The sociologist Miroslav Jodl, for example, called the signatories 'traitors' and their letter a 'stab in the back'. He suggested that they should 'emigrate to where they seek support and find response'.[27] This does raise the question of 'public support'.

As 'Czechoslovakia 1968' was about reforming a socialist system, and as the working class was estimated to have constituted 58 per cent of the population, their attitude was important. Surprisingly, the working class showed no great interest in the reform movement. Their initial reaction has been described as 'indifferent', indeed even hostile. They were suspicious because of the strong intellectual basis of the reform movement and Novotny, during January and February, was able to draw large audiences to meetings at which he criticised the January decisions. This suspicion did not ease in subsequent months. As late as May 1968 the majority of workers were very sceptical about the attempted reforms.[28] As far as local party branches were concerned, they did not turn up for branch meetings. It was not until the invasion of August 1968, when a completely new situation had arisen, that the bulk of the working population clearly threw in their lot with the harassed Dubcek Government. As far as the rest of the population was concerned, the situation was similar. Novotny was credited with having 'enjoyed substantial support, primarily in the apparatus but also in the army and police, the state bureaucracy and even among the broad masses'.[29] This demanded a careful and gradual approach in explaining the necessity of his removal. As Skilling points out, no one reads the mind of the broad masses. But although the reforms had received plenty of discussion in the media, by February the 'masses'' mind was not overly concerned with the 'deepening of socialist democracy'. When asked which was the most urgent problem to be solved, three-quarters of the responses referred to various economic shortcomings. The deepening of socialist democracy was in seventh place, with less than 5 per cent of the survey listing this as the top priority.[30]

Reactions to the April action programme were generally favourable, although a survey undertaken shortly after its publication showed that only 16 per cent had read the programme in its entirety; 25 per cent had read some of it and 35 per cent received their knowledge through the news media. Some 18 per cent knew about it only from hearsay and 6 per cent did not know it at all. Another opinion poll supported the principle that the leading role of the Communist Party should be upheld. Hence there was no widespread support for 'pluralism' or Westernisation. Although the limitations of these opinion polls have been pointed out, they have nevertheless played a great part in the writings of Western analysts. Some of the polls[31] do present interesting material.

Question: Would you prefer that Czechoslovakia relinquish the building of Communism and enter the way of capitalist development, or do you wish to continue building socialism?

	Per cent
1. I prefer capitalist development	5
2. I am for the continuation of socialist development	89
3. I do not know, I have not thought about it	6
	100

These figures do not support the myth still propagated in the Anglo-Saxon press and television empires that the intervention in Czechoslovakia in 1968 saw the defeat of a return to Western democracy. Nor did the polls show that the Czech and Slovak people had turned anti-Soviet. They were eager to continue their friendship with the Soviet Union.[32]

That the opinions and policies of the intellectuals were not unanimously shared by the public is shown in a survey undertaken in May. Asked 'would you consider the present process of democratisation to be beneficial' just over half answered this question in the affirmative. But 21 per cent felt that it was beneficial to the intelligentsia and not to the common people. To a further 19 per cent, the present changes were ineffective and 4 per cent went even further and felt that it was not beneficial to anyone and hurt everyone.[33]

Nor did the reforms cause any immediate change in the healthy distrust the Czechs and Slovaks held towards politics and politicians. Asked whether they regarded politics as 'dirty', 40 per cent answered yes, 38 per cent no. Some 47 per cent agreed that politicians were seeking their own advancement. And as the following survey[34] about television viewing undertaken in April shows, most preferred a hefty scandal story.

When you remember what you have read recently in the newspapers, heard on the radio, or seen on television, which articles or broadcasts regarding the development of internal politics are you not likely to forget? (in per cent)

	All	Czech lands	Slovakia
The evening discussion with youth transmitted by radio and television	17.2	19.1	12.5
Speeches and articles of individuals who contributed to democratisation	15.0	15.1	14.9
Rehabilitation, imprisonment, interrogation and trials of innocents	9.6	10.6	6.8
The Sejna affair[35]	52.2	49.5	59.2
Others	6.0	5.7	6.6
	100.0	100.0	100.0

Another survey discussed political problems that should be dealt with by the news media. Most respondents felt that too much was said about the mistakes of the past and not enough about what to do in the future.[36] When the delegates to the Fourteenth Party Congress were asked what was the greatest threat to the current reform course, 63.8 per cent nominated anti-socialism and 65.8 per cent saw 'conservative' elements as the main threat.[37] New political parties did not gain great popularity. The political club KAN, which claimed to be a spokesman for the non-communist majority of the nation, had only a few thousand members. As such it fared worse than the already existing non-communist parties, normally not mentioned in Western accounts because of their alleged 'satellite' status, which nevertheless considerably increased their membership during 1968. The Czechoslovak People's Party (CSL) rose from 20,642 members on 1 January 1968 to 46,028 on 1 July of that year. The corresponding figures for the Czechoslovak Socialist Party were 10,715 and 17,323.[38] The public opinion pollsters also tried to find out who would have won a Western-style election.[39]

Voting in Elections this Month (in percentages)

Respondents would vote for:	
Communist Party	43
Socialist Party	13
People's Party	9
Blank ballot, don't know, or no answer	33
	98

One third did not answer, and no explanation is provided for why they did not give a preference. If the conventional Western opinion poll methods are applied to this result (to distribute the 'don't knows' according to the percentage), the Communist Party would have scored just under 70 per cent. Opinion polls about the occupation naturally showed that the great majority of the Czech and Slovak people rejected it.

Essentially the Czechoslovak reform movement was centred on intellectuals and affiliated sections of the community like writers and journalists. And although, as the thinkers, they play a vital part in the functioning of a nation, they are numerically only a small part of the population and their thoughts and actions are not necessarily shared by the rest of the community. In fact, as has been shown by some of the opinion polls, and as has been confirmed by sociological research in Eastern Europe, popular concepts are often critical of and opposed to intellectuals, a fact which is also true for the West. This should have suggested to the pro-reform section that if they hoped to succeed they should step more carefully and gradually to ensure that the new policies were in fact widely supported. But of this there was little sign in the Czechoslovak reform movement. Instead there was wide-ranging confusion and virtually no competent leadership. By the time crowds of people were roaring through Prague at night, shouting anti-Soviet slogans and attacking public buildings, by the time there were calls from high-ranking sections of the army to withdraw from the Warsaw Pact, by the time the 'Kremlin-Round' of the extremely right-wing Second West German Television was broadcast from Prague, featuring such famous 'Kremlinologists' as Z. Brzezinski,[40] by that time what looked to the West and Western-orientated sections of the Czechoslovakian intelligentsia, politicians and population as a beautiful spring was to most socialists in Eastern Europe – and not only to the 'hard-liners' – a miserable grey autumn of petty-bourgeois social democratic revisionism. On 20 August, Soviet, Polish, GDR, Hungarian and Bulgarian troops occupied the CSSR.

A great deal had been written about what may have prompted the final decision. The West German 'revanchist' policies have played an important part in the explanations presented by both sides. It is true that the Hallstein doctrine which was particularly directed against Poland and the GDR had been a key part of the FRG foreign policy. With the advent of Willy Brandt this was beginning to change, although the full impact of his policies may not have been recognised by the Eastern Europeans. Yet while one should not underplay the overall importance of 'West Germany' in the 1968 crisis, it is hard to believe that Eastern military strategists really felt that the FRG would strike at Czechoslovakia. The West Germans were in no military position to do so with their own forces and there would have been no allied — especially no US — support. Nor does there seem to have been a compelling domestic reason for the invasion. The composition of the Fourteenth Party Congress does not hint that the radical pro-reform sections would have gained the upper hand. On the other hand, for the Eastern leaders to take such a drastic step there must have been a compelling reason to offset the damage such an event would cause. It would certainly confirm the conventional picture of the Eastern Bloc in the West and the growing support the Soviet Union and her allies were gaining among the Third World countries would be greatly jeopardised. Yet above all it would seriously hurt the friendship with the Czech and Slovak nation, which had been a long-standing and reliable ally. They must obviously have feared that the forces drawing the CSSR into pluralism and Western democracy were strong enough to do so and so did some members of the Czechoslovak Communist Party who asked for Soviet intervention. It is beyond the scope of this book to judge whether there was a realistic chance of the CSSR leaving the socialist world. But the strategic blow of such a step to Eastern Europe would have been so disastrous that it would have outweighed the damage done by the occupation.

Soviet troops occupied Prague, but as far as the rest of the nation was concerned it amounted to little more than an occupation in support of international socialism. The Bulgarians sent a mere token force which had to be flown in as Romania refused to participate in the occupation. The GDR's part in the operation was a particularly delicate issue because of the German march into that country 30 years previously. The whole GDR involvement amounted to little more than a small contingent of troops crossing the borders and virtually hiding in a nearby forest. In a subsequent attempt to justify the events the Soviets later published a document, known as the Brezhnev doctrine, which stated that notwithstanding the principle of national integrity, socialist internationalism may over-ride the principle of nationalism. Not surprisingly this document has been labelled as a blue-print for Soviet intervention and it must be noted that the strong emphasis on national independence was a concept which the founding fathers of socialism and all early theoreticians rejected as a bourgeois middle-class concept. Even Rosa Luxemburg had argued that the concept of self-determination and nationalism was a product of capitalism, a relic from the bourgeois age not fitted for socialism.[41] Since her time, the international power constellation has changed radically and, in the wake of Stalin, the national road to socialism rivals claims of international solidarity. The extremely careful stance the Soviet Union has taken on this issue since 1968 — as shown at the moment with the Polish problem — seems to confirm that nationalism gained even more ground during the 1970s.

Understandably the reaction in East and West to the occupation was extreme. The people resented the occupation, yet to speak of 'resistance rare in human experience'[42] seems far-fetched. If it was, it must have been in the hearts and minds of the people, as there were few actions. There was a one-hour strike on 19 August at 12.00 noon in which almost the whole workforce participated. Otherwise the situation returned to normal. To judge from the opinion polls there was no 'endless gloom'. An opinion poll in September revealed that only 14.4 per cent of the people believed that the Soviet troops would stay forever.[43]

With the occupation by the five Warsaw Pact countries, the case for the reformists was lost. Dubcek carried on for a further eight months before he was replaced by Gustav Husak who, like Kadar 13 years previously, tried to steer a centre course between the warring factions. Dubcek was not put on trial but his social position took a steep dive. His Rolls Royce, equipped with refrigerated bar and television, was returned to the manufacturers in Derby.[44] Throughout the 1970s Husak's government stabilised the economy, improved the standard of living and liberalised restraints on citizens' visits to the West. But he failed to bridge the deep divide between the party and a considerable section of the Czech intelligentsia.

Notes and References

1. Concluded in December 1943 between Stalin and the exiled Czech President Eduart Benes.
2. Quoted in Jan M. Michal, *Central Planning in Czechoslovakia* (Stanford University Press, 1960), pp. 48-51.
3. Ibid., p. 198.
4. Theodor Bermann, *Farm Policies in Socialist Countries* (Saxon House, Farnborough, 1975), p. 79.
5. Ibid., pp. 80-1.
6. See above, pp. 83-4.
7. Miloslav Bernasek, 'The Czechoslovak Economic Recession, 1962-65', *Soviet Studies*, vol. XX, no. 4 (1969), p. 455.
8. Ibid., p. 460.
9. Josef C. Brada, 'The Czechoslovak Economic Recession, 1962-65: Comment', *Soviet Studies*, vol. 22 (1971), p. 402.
10. Ibid., p. 403.
11. Ibid., pp. 404-5.
12. E. Taborsky 'Czechoslovakia out of Stalinism', *Problems of Communism*,

vol. 13, no. 3, pp. 5-13.
13. Ibid., p. 13.
14. Steele, *Socialism in Eastern Europe*, p. 161.
15. Rudolf Bahro, *The Alternative in Eastern Europe* (NLB, London, 1978).
16. Sik, *Problems of Peace and Socialism*, quoted in Steele, *Socialism in Eastern Europe*, pp. 136-7.
17. H. Gordon Skilling, *Czechoslovakia's Interrupted Revolution* (Princeton University Press, 1976), p. 415.
18. Vladimir V. Kusin, *The Intellectual Origins of the Prague Spring* (Cambridge University Press, London, 1971), p. 85.
19. Ibid., pp. 63-7.
20. Milan Kundera, 'Speech at the 4th Writers' Congress' quoted in Kusin, ibid., p. 74.
21. A.J. Liehm, 'Speech at the 4th Writers' Congress' quoted in Kusin, ibid., p. 74.
22. Ibid., p. 137.
23. Ibid., pp. 112-13.
24. See above, pp. 107-9.
25. Quoted in Skilling, *Czechoslovakia's Interrupted Revolution*, p. 357.
26. For details, see Steele, *Socialism in Eastern Europe*, pp. 165 ff.
27. Skilling, *Czechoslovakia's Interrupted Revolution*, pp. 324-5.
28. Alex Pravda, 'Some aspects of the Czechoslovak economic reform and the working class in 1968' in *Soviet Studies*, vol. 25, no. 1 (1973), p. 110. 36 per cent thought things got worse before they got better, 37 per cent were undecided.
29. Ibid., p. 161.
30. Skilling, *Czechoslovakia's Interrupted Revolution*, pp. 534-5.
31. Jaroslav A. Piekalkiewicz, *Public Opinion Polling in Czechoslovakia* (Praeger, London, 1972), p. 4.
32. Skilling, *Czechoslovakia's Interrupted Revolution*, p. 651.
33. Piekalkiewicz, *Public Opinion Polling*, p. 95.
34. Piekalkiewicz, ibid., p. 38.
35. Jan Sejna was a General in the CSSR army who defected to the United States in February 1968 with his son and a young woman. He was about to be arrested on the charge of embezzlement of state property. He was believed to be a close friend of Novotny and the fact that the police could not prevent him crossing into Hungary (from where he proceeded to Yugoslavia and then the United States) caused something of a sensation in Czechoslovakia.
36. Piekalkiewicz, *Public Opinion Polling*, p. 95.
37. Skilling, *Czechoslovakia's Interrupted Revolution*, p. 512.
38. Ibid., pp. 452 ff.
39. Ibid., p. 546.
40. The later foreign adviser to the Carter administration.
41. *Neue Zeit*, vol. 1, 'The Nation State and the Proletariat, 1897-8'.
42. Skilling, *Czechoslovakia's Interrupted Revolution*, p. 809.
43. Piekalkiewicz, *Public Opinion Polling*, p. 58.
44. *Daily Telegraph*, 17 Feb. 1983, p. 3.

8 THE POLISH PEOPLE'S REPUBLIC: CATHOLICS AND CULTIVATORS

In the winter of 1966-7 the British journalist William Woods was approached by a representative of the Polish government and asked whether he would visit and write a book about contemporary Poland. The government felt that the West knew too little about Poland.

Woods was promised every possible co-operation: travel would be unrestricted and he could talk to whomever he liked and, of course, write what he pleased. The Poles did ask him, however, to look at his task in the perspective of Polish history, with an awareness of Poland's particular economic and political problems and write as fairly and objectively as he was able. Woods took up the offer and presented his findings in an interesting book[1] which presents a far more informative picture of modern-day Poland than is found in the standard Western academic publications. 'The socialist government', writes Woods, 'found there were two problems they would never solve satisfactorily without enormous patience. One was their relationship with the Church, the other with the peasantry who formed the Church's staunch pillar.'[2] After almost four decades it does not appear that the government has solved either.

History had not been kind to Poland or the Poles. From being a formidable power in Europe in the sixteenth and seventeenth centuries (in fact *the* leading power in Eastern Europe), Poland had disappeared as an independent state by the end of the eighteenth century. Historians of early modern history attribute this to a number of factors, of which aggression by hostile neighbours was only one. Economic, political and social backwardness played an equally important, if not more important, part in explaining the ability of Russia, Prussia and Austria to divide and eventually swallow up the country. Centralisation of political power, on the ascendant everywhere in Europe, was virtually non-existent in Poland. Instead the country was dominated by a small clique of nobles and operated under conditions of virtual anarchy. The small privileged section of the country so exploited its rural dwellers that there were no major armed forces to rely on when the foreign powers descended upon the country. Contemporary travellers claimed that Poland had the most deplorable living conditions of all Europe. And as Europe in the eighteenth century was not known for signs of

The Polish People's Republic

general affluence, this claim speaks for itself. Archdeacon Coxe, travelling through Europe, wrote that the Poles 'are sunk in blackest poverty and are abysmally ignorant, they are huddled with their cattle in clusters of ramshackle wooden villages along muddy roads which are impassable save in summer'.[3]

After two partitions in the second half of the eighteenth century, Poland disappeared from the map. It was partly as a result of such blunt acts of power politics, partly as a consequence of the new nationalism that emerged in Europe during the nineteenth century that the agitation to become an independent state never ceased. 'Poland is not lost as yet', became their national anthem and the hopes for independence were kept alive throughout the nineteenth century. With the collapse of all of the former partitioners in 1917-18, Poland rose once more as a national state and was given recognition at Versailles in 1919. Yet in 1939 Poland was again divided. It would not be fair or accurate to level too much blame about the abysmal end of the Polish Republic upon the people who created and ran the nation. They too were victims of the post-First World War power constellation. However, it would also be factually incorrect to allege that the bulk of the Polish population after 1945 looked with favour on the West or yearned for the old political system which had been incapable of avoiding the Second World War catastrophe. Yet the new social and economic order did not end the cycle of crises which have characterised Poland's history. For notwithstanding the more spectacular events of Hungary in 1956 and Czechoslovakia in 1968, the People's Republic of Poland above all Eastern European states followed the most trouble-stricken course. Continuous stages of economic crises were too often followed by social confrontation as well.

The initial start to the post-Second World War period was very promising. Ethnically and economically the new Poland was a far more viable proposition than the former Polish Republic. The loss of the backward agricultural parts in the east – where the Polish element was in a minority – was well compensated for by the acquisition of Silesia – a fertile country with advanced industries – and the former German port of Danzig, which became Gdansk. Aided by the far-reaching economic reforms, especially the redistribution of land during 1946-7, the Polish community faced the huge task of reconstructing the war-torn country with some degree of enthusiasm. As was the case in the neighbouring socialist countries, the massive industrialisation drive of the early long-term plans had somewhat weakened this elan by the mid-1950s, and the first clash between rebellious workers and government forces eight years after the establishment of the People's Republic in 1948 was spectacular. The Poznan strike of late June 1956 is said to have begun at the Stalin Locomotive Works in that city, with demands initially centring upon better working conditions and improvements in living standards. It quickly snowballed into a fully-fledged confrontation between demonstrators and troops stationed nearby in which 53 people were killed and about 300 injured.

Western accounts present the Poznan riots as a clear indication of working-class spontaneity. The 'other side' pointed to the activity of Western agents who had come to the city in the wake of an international trade fair held at that time and to the fact that the United States government had recently increased its budget to support forces aiding democracy in Eastern Europe by 25 million dollars. With the benefit of hindsight the Eastern European claim of undercover activity in support of anti-socialist forces in their countries is not a mere fabrication and one may safely assume that the real cause of events lies somewhere between the two presentations. But even without the Poznan riots, changes in the Polish government were imminent.

The de-Stalinisation drive of the mid-1950s had created a situation which demanded change. There had already been several months of confrontation within the Polish United Workers' Party, both in the plenum of the Central Committee and in the Politbureau. The forces demanding radical changes in the policies and leadership of the party were gradually getting the upper hand and on 21 October 1956, Wladyslaw Gomulka was elected First Secretary of the Central Committee. Gomulka was highly popular. Fifty-one years of age and of working-class background, he was an old communist who had fought with the Polish underground and in the post-war years he stood for the national path of socialism, for which he was imprisoned in the purges of the late 1940s and early 1950s. He returned to a hero's welcome as his popularity spread well beyond the realm of the party. Nor did Gomulka initially fail to live up to the high expectations held of him. He immediately set out to improve the strained relationship with the Polish Catholic Church and with the other two political parties. He introduced a series of liberal reforms and a little later halted the implementation of collectivist farming policies.

The liberal reforms especially were widely noted. The US-based journal *Problems of Communism*, quoting a Warsaw newspaper in early 1957, stated that 'A spectre is haunting Eastern Europe — the spectre of human socialism — and it frightens not only the capitalists but also the Stalinists.'[4] Although this initial jubilation softened over the next couple of years, liberalisation of the arts in Eastern Europe commenced in Poland, and in principle continued throughout Gomulka's time and the Gierek years, as can be seen by the nature of Polish literature, theatre and film over the last generation.

Liberalisation of Poland's cultural life was an important aspect of Gomulka's early policies but more important were the economic reforms and improvements in living conditions. In its initial five-year plan the Gomulka Government concentrated upon consumer goods, although during the latter stages of this plan emphasis shifted again to higher investment levels for heavy industry. This brought some notable achievements. The production of raw materials, especially coal, copper and sulphur, showed huge increases. Poland became the second largest exporter of sulphur. Iron and steel production also rose and there were particularly steep rises in the output of chemical products and electricity. William Woods's description of Polish industrial centres in the mid-1960s shows impressive achievements. But by this time the familiar problems had resurfaced. Although Polish economic theoreticians were among the first to point to the dilemma posed by the change from extensive to intensive production, the Gomulka Government refused to revitalise Poland's economic policies and preferred to continue along the traditional economic path. This lead to a steady deterioration of the Polish economy in the late 1960s. A Western economist observed that Polish industry had not been able to adapt its output to changing patterns of industrial and consumer demands. Much of Poland's substantially expanding output was said to have ended up as unwanted inventory gathering dust in the nation's warehouses.[5] By the end of 1970 it was estimated that inventories increased at twice the rate of retail sales growth to total half of the 1970 Polish gross national product. Living standards remained low and at the same time there was pronounced neglect of working conditions. Low rises in the standard of living affected in particular the less well to do. Table 8.1 shows, with indices of growth rates between 1965 and 1970 (1965 = 100), that real earnings for Poland had fallen behind the other socialist countries.[6] Thus although on the surface everything seemed in order − with apparently little conflict between the Polish government, the Church and intellectuals − underneath discontent was smouldering.

The situation was aggravated by the crisis in the agricultural sector. The abandonment of the collectivist programme did not lead to lasting permanent improvements in agricultural production. Attempts to modernise output through the formation of so-called 'agricultural-circles' did not get very far. These circles did not affect the private ownership of land and the farmers were supposed to join together in a co-operative for communal buying of machinery and the joint use of the machines. Hence these circles resembled Western agricultural co-operatives but as there was no pressure to join, by the mid-1960s only one fourth of the holdings belonged to them. Bad climatic conditions and a poor harvest added fuel to the crisis and the decision of the Gomulka Government to raise basic food prices and prices for other staples by up to 20 per cent led to strikes and protests in a number of Polish cities, especially those along the Baltic coast. At the end of 1970 in Gdansk armed forces are said to have killed 36 workers and injured several hundreds. It was this brutal handling of the affair which led to Gomulka's dismissal as First Secretary of the party and his replacement by Eduard Gierek.

Table 8.1: Growth Rates of Retail Earnings in Selected Socialist Countries, 1965-70

Yugoslavia	141
Bulgaria	130
USSR	122
CSSR	120
Romania	120
Hungary	118
Poland	111

Gierek had been in the forefront of the party for several years. He was of genuine proletarian origins, the son of a Silesian coal-miner who died in a mine accident, and Gierek himself had worked in the mines in his youth. He joined the United Polish Workers' Party in 1948 and between 1957 and 1970 he served as Secretary of the Katowice Provincial Committee. In this time he earned a reputation as a first-class administrator which led to his election to succeed Gomulka in December 1970. Like Gomulka, Gierek had a long-standing record of fighting for the cause of socialism. He was expelled from France in 1934 for participating in a miners' strike and later went to Belgium where he became active in the communist movement before he returned to Poland in 1948.[7]

Gierek replaced the party leadership with a group of younger men and he began immediately to give the Polish economy a more consumerist direction. The new policy was to be 'based on the fundamental idea that the highest goal of socialism lies in the constant satisfaction of the material and spiritual needs of the people on the basis of dynamic economic development'.[8] The new pragmatic policies rested on the principle that hard work properly rewarded was to be the mainspring of economic progress: 'Increased consumption is an important and necessary factor in the process of economic growth, a factor which stimulates production and technological progress, improves organization and results in greater labour productivity.'[9]

Attempts were also made to cut down on waste and inefficiency. Thus there was no major 'new economic policy' but an improved version of the old policies. There was a huge increase in the range of available consumer goods over the following years and the living standards of the Polish people by the mid-1970s had clearly risen. Most of this improvement, however, was not brought about by a rise in production but by massive foreign loans from both the East and West. Loans from the West in particular grew out of all proportion (see Table 8.2).

Table 8.2: Loans from the West (1976)

	$
USSR	18,000m
Poland	12,000m
GDR	7,000m
Romania	3,500m
Hungary	3,000m
Bulgaria	3,000m
Czechoslovakia	2,000m
Comecon banks	2,100m
Total	$50,600m

Poland had the highest borrowing rate in relation to the size of its economy — much higher than the economically advanced GDR — and the Polish loans were high in relation to the growth of productivity. Western loans were expensive and a strain upon the nation's hard currency reserves. By the mid-1970s the pinch was being felt. The time of relative prosperity was obviously over and in 1976 there were again confrontations with sections of the workforce over planned price rises. By now it had become clear that, notwithstanding initial advances, the problems of the Polish economy had not been solved. In fact the seemingly never-ending economic *misère* began to affect life and society as a whole. By now all news coming out of Poland seemed to be of a negative nature. The Western-based periodicals on Eastern Europe in the mid-1970s did occasionally present material which did not fall into the 'problems of Communism' bracket and in fact showed that some countries in some fields had been making real progress. But the stories from Poland were getting ever more depressing: in addition to neverending economic setbacks there were shortcomings and problems in schools, universities, health and housing. The alcohol problem was alleged to have grown out of all proportion. No Eastern European state and very few of the Western European states are credited with modest drinking habits, but the proverbial saying in Eastern Europe, 'Drunk as a Pole', does hint at an already high level of alcohol consumption which even increased in the 1970s. The only positive development Western observers could see in Poland was an emerging anti-socialist movement strongly supported by some Polish Catholics. This group was tolerated by the government although it advocated a return to the pre-1945 political system.[10] Then in 1980, just before the completion of a decade of Gierek Government, the situation exploded with the formation of the Solidarity union.

Writing at the peak of the crisis in 1981, the Romanian leader Ceaucescu, who is not known for a particularly 'conformist' approach in his comments about conditions in Eastern Europe, pointed to the hopeless state of Polish agriculture as the real source of all the problems. It is difficult to dismiss the validity of this claim. Although for a number of years Polish agriculture had been lavishly praised by Western writers for not having adopted the co-operative system, Eastern European style, visitors to the country were frequently struck by the backwardness of the countryside. Williams Woods, travelling in 1967 in the coastal country near Szczecin, gave this unflattering account:

Whatever the reason, the villages round about are ramshackle places too, with tins, broken bottles, and scraps of paper littering the unattended gardens, with their few orchards gone to ruin, their very churches derelict, their peasants often still barefooted and almost invariably unshaved, with cottages that have holes in their roofs, scraggy hens fluttering in and out through their broken windows, with dirt and idleness visible wherever one looks.

I spent a whole day wandering from hamlet to hamlet along this frontier. Here a farmer who admitted with a shrug that he never got out into the fields until noon. There a young woman sitting in a doorway, gazing lackadaisically at her feet. Normally she woke at nine when the baby cried. What was the use of getting up earlier? The more one did the more there was to do. In the next farmyard, a grandmother in the nearest thing possible to rags, her face and neck seamy with accumulated filth.[11]

This may have been rock-bottom, but such conditions were repeated throughout the Polish countryside.[12] Visiting Poland a few years later, a German contributor to the *Osteuropa* periodical gave this account:

> All the time we come across horse carriages. Like in old landscape paintings there are hills on the horizon, peasants ploughing work horses, a kind of scene which has almost disappeared from our minds. Hardly even eight per cent of the sowing work and less than thirty per cent of the harvesting are done by machines . . . the distribution of fields makes it clear that Poland is a small peasant based country . . . It seems difficult for the western observer to believe that such a system of land distribution, which is in part accompanied by overpopulation, will remain forever.[13]

And when the British economic historian Alec Nove visited the country in the late 1970s, he had this to say:

> As any visitor to Poland can see, fields are small, many peasant households have 5 hectares of land or less, which is scarcely conducive to mechanisation, and I saw myself literally dozens of peasants sowing by throwing seed into the wind by hand. Productivity per head cannot be other than low, and it is arguable that further gains in yields are improbable without some major structural changes.[14]

By the mid-1970s there were still 2½ million horses in Poland (compared to about 76,000 in the GDR or 163,000 in Hungary). As Nove correctly points out, horses eat grain — which explains Poland's grain deficit. This deficit continues to grow.

As Table 8.3 shows, although Poland produces more grain than the GDR, its imports have risen above the latter's. In Poland, one third of the population are still employed in agriculture and forestry compared to 11.5 per cent in the GDR. Poland's export meat market has been expanding, but this has caused domestic shortages. These figures invalidate the notion of the 'healthy Polish private agriculture' — as opposed to the 'collectivised system' — an image which still prevails in the writings of some political writers who base their claim not so much on factual material as upon wishful thinking. Other factors such as the drift to the cities by young people, which has greatly increased the average age of the rural population, have added to the problems facing Poland. So did the government's periodic failure to provide sufficient fertilisers and/or machinery. The last problem is not confined to Poland, although it may be more pronounced here, and is not the key to the Polish agricultural malaise.

Table 8.3:[15] Foreign Trade in Grain (1970-75) ('000 tons)

		1970	1971	1972	1973	1974	1975
Bulgaria	(export)	462	558	833	367	149	195
	(import)	158	195	–	136	637	653
Hungary	(export)	810	112	505	1,732	1,472	1,285
	(import)	181	808	789	265	390	172
GDR	(import)	3,424	3,066	3,845	2,990	2,770	3,360
Poland	(export)	200	111	208	410	262	104
	(import)	2,484	2,950	3,108	3,263	4,091	3,963
Romania	(export)[a]	370	702	900	1,026	711	1,163
Czechoslovakia	(import)	1,439	2,033	1,550	1,552	1,038	885
USSR	(export)			4,560	4,853	7,029	3,578
	(import)			15,500	23,900	7,131	15,909

(a) Wheat plus maize only

However, the Poles do not only have to supplement their food needs by massive imports simply because of the grain consumption by horses. Polish soil is not exceptionally fertile, but both Hungary and Bulgaria had to import food before the Second World War, although they have both been able to eradicate their dependency upon food imports and indeed provide a surplus for export by modernising their agriculture. Such an achievement by the Poles would not only have closed the trade deficit but also have brought in hard currency. Yet the losses in agriculture have had to be made up by gains in industry — valuable valuta which could be used for consumer goods, for example, had been dissipated. The Polish workers were affected by the agrarian crisis in two ways: first, it limited the returns for their labour, as the range of goods Polish workers could buy was very restricted; secondly, as part of the Polish agricultural production is used for export, the workers' share in meat and food distribution has been traditionally modest. Well before the events of 1981, it was common knowledge in Eastern Europe 'that you don't get much to eat in Poland'.

Nove is quite right. These shortages are due to a price policy dictated by politics not by economic sense. Polish money wages have risen in the period 1967-75 by over 60 per cent, whereas the prices of livestock products have been frozen. Attempts to increase them in December 1970 and in June 1976 and in 1980 have been frustrated by mass protests.

Hence the extremely heavy subsidies on meat. It was not until the proclamation of martial law that the government, under pressure from Western creditors, announced hefty price increases. The previous economic policies indeed made no economic sense, but having had to bear the brunt of the faulty Polish economic system it was natural that the Polish workers protested at the threat to stable food prices. They have been paying the price for the mistakes in the Polish economy for a long time − not surprisingly, the pressure resulted in the founding of an organisation to defend their interests. The establishment of Solidarity is a fitting comment on the Polish economy.

The formation of Solidarity and, subsequently, the principle of its right to exist, soon became an emotional catchword for conservative Western statesmen who in their own country have a reputation as 'union bashers'. Understandable as the move towards Solidarity was, it is still questionable whether it was a move towards progressive socialism, as has been maintained by sections of the Western left. The original idea of the union movement − to represent the interests of the workers in their struggle against the power and economic strength of the employers − should in theory be an alien concept in a socialist society. That groups of vested interests are set against each other is not an idea found in any theories of socialist society. Likewise, in the capitalist orbit it became obvious during the 1970s that in those countries where the emphasis in employer-employee relations was not on confrontation but on cooperation (such as Sweden, Japan and West Germany), the economic performance profited. By contrast, where a more traditional 'here employer, here employee' attitude prevailed (as in Britain and Australia), the economy experienced a far greater slump in the trouble-stricken 1970s. Thus while the creation of Solidarity is understandable in the light of Poland's economic history, the step can hardly be described as a great advance towards a socialist society. As is known, the Gierek Government fell over its handling of the economy. Its successors gave in on a wide range of contentious issues − in fact, they leaned over backwards to come to an all-round agreement. Nevertheless confrontations continued, grew more frequent, and further damaged the struggling Polish economy. Each side blamed the other for breaking the agreements until the emergency decrees of December 1981 put a temporary end to the reforms.

So the problem of Poland has not been solved. A basic revision of agriculture would be the key, although it is of course not the only factor. The level of debts and the Polish price system added to the downturn. Other issues such as waste and corruption would have added their share although the extent can only be guessed at. Embezzlement and associated crimes are a problem in all the socialist countries, yet their precise role is not easy to determine nor is it possible to state whether such factors were more pronounced in Poland than elsewhere. But this should not detract from the basic non-viability of the Polish economic system.

Agricultural reforms have played a dominant part in Polish economic theory and at party conventions for many years. But it seems difficult to point to a way out. Modernisation of the small-scale farms, which certain Western commentators proposed during the 1980-1 crisis, is not viable.[16] Some Western European countries, notably France, have developed such a system within the European Economic Community, but at great economic cost. The CMEA countries are not as wealthy as their Western neighbours and in any case France's rural scene was historically more advanced than that of Poland. Another Western model, large modernised farms of the British variety, might overcome the current stalemate. However, the disadvantage of this lies in the fact that the existence of a class of prosperous large landowners is not particularly welcome in a socialist country. Furthermore, this option would not end the plight of the old peasants who see their system of agriculture disappearing. The GDR or Hungarian co-operative system seems the most logical way out, but this solution is impossible in the current political climate.

Today the Polish problem has spread well beyond Poland. Most people and statesmen on both sides in Europe, still remembering the last war, maintain a position of non-intervention, encouraging the Poles themselves to solve their problems. But such a commendable stance is not universal. Poland is the Achilles heel of the Eastern European states. Some cynical observers commented that the decision of the Catholic Church to appoint a Pole as Pope, the first non-Italian in more than 500 years, was an attempt to rub salt into Polish wounds. Yet, no doubt the Catholic Church is interested in maintaining peace and does not want the issue to lead to a new and disastrous confrontation. This is more than one can say for the Reagan administration in the United States, which has made Poland the focus of its anti-Soviet crusade. Yet neither the burning of candles at night nor Frank Sinatra singing in Polish will solve the Polish problem.

The old anthem is still current: Poland is not lost as yet. But it is not far from it.

Notes and References

1. William Woods, *Poland: Eagle in the East: a Survey of Modern Times* (Deutsch, London, 1968), p. 178.
2. Ibid., p. 178.
3. Leo Gershoy, 'From Despotism to Revolution, 1763-89' (Harper and Brothers, London, 1953), pp. 37-8.
4. *Przelglad Kulturalny*, 7 Nov. 1956, quoted in *Problems of Communism*, vol. 6 (1957), p. 1.
5. Michael Gamarnikow, 'A New Economic Approach', *Problems of Communism*, vol. 20, no. 5 (1971), p. 21.
6. Zygmunt Kozslowski, 'Gierek missglücktes Wirtschaftswunder', *Osteuropa*, vol. 28 (1978), p. 623.
7. Adam Bromke, 'Poland under Gierek. A New Political Style', *Problems of Communism*, vol. 21, no. 5 (1972), p. 6.
8. Quoted in Gamarnikow, 'A New Economic Approach', p. 24.
9. Ibid.
10. For details see Adam Bromke, 'The Opposition in Poland', *Problems of Communism*, vol. 27, no. 5 (1978), pp. 37-51.
11. Woods, *Poland*, pp. 122-3.
12. Ibid.
13. Harold Lauen, 'Reise durch Polen', *Osteuropa*, vol. 23 (1973), pp. 768-9.
14. Aleo Nove, *Political Economy and Soviet Socialism* (Allen and Unwin, London, 1979), p. 168.
15. Ibid.
16. Tadeusz Szafar, 'Die Dekade Gierek', *Osteuropa*, vol. 13 (1981), pp. 283-4; Z. Kozlowski, *Osteuropa*, vol. 12 (1980), pp. 1285-1302.

9 YUGOSLAVIA: COMMUNIST LEAGUE AND WORKERS' COUNCILS

The funeral of the Yugoslav President Jozip Broz, called Tito, on Thursday 8 May 1980, was one of the most momentous occasions of recent years. In addition to millions of his countrymen, the heads of state and prime ministers of more than 100 nations, including the American President Carter and the Soviet leader Leonid Brezhnev, attended to pay a last tribute to a man who had become a legend in his own lifetime. Tito was born in 1893 and grew up in Zagorje, between Slovenia and Croatia. He started out as a bellboy, worked for a few years in the Ruhr, the major German industrial region, and was a driver for Daimler in Vienna before he fought for Austria-Hungary in the First World War. On returning in 1920 from a Russian prisoner-of-war camp he joined the Yugoslav communist movement, which he headed by the outbreak of the Second World War. During the war he led the partisans against the German occupation and by the end of the war his forces had not only contributed significantly to the defeat of the fascists but had also supplanted his internal opponents. For the next 35 years he ruled Yugoslavia placing his individual stamp on the nation's political life until he finally became the spokesman for the non-aligned world, a symbol of political neutrality and integrity.

There was much speculation in both the East and the West about the post-Tito course. Would it be possible to continue with that country's independent course or would Yugoslavia now become closely aligned to one or other of the superpowers and, if so, which one? Tito's successors had inherited a distinguished record in the area of foreign policy. However, the domestic record was not nearly as impressive. After more than a generation of Workers' Councils and the League of Communists, Yugoslavia faced many problems.

The split between Yugoslavia and the Soviet Union with her Eastern European allies in 1949 struck at the very basis of the new Yugoslav economy. At that time, 50 per cent of Yugoslavia's trade was with her socialist neighbours and an even greater part of the planned import of industrial equipment was to come from that source. Yugoslavia's trade deficit rose tenfold between 1948 and 1950 and the need to raise the defence budget to one quarter of the total budget added to the problems. A severe drought during 1950 caused further difficulties. Not surprisingly, therefore, at a time when the other socialist countries were achieving impressive growth rates (at least in some fields), industrial production in Yugoslavia was stagnant for several years.

Nevertheless, Tito and the Yugoslav communist leadership decided to make a 'sweeping break' with the course pursued during the immediate post-war years. Soon laws were passed to allow for a shift away from centralist organisation of administration. In May 1949 a Law on People's Committees gave greater economic and political power to organs of self-government.[1] In that year too several central economic ministries were replaced by councils at the federal and republic level. Also, and most importantly, it was in 1949 that the first experiments in worker's self-management were introduced.

In December 1949, 200 large enterprises established advisory bodies which had worker representation. In June 1950 the Yugoslav Federal Assembly passed the first law on worker's self-management, the Basic Law, which made it obligatory for industrial enterprises with more than 30 employers to implement elections to Workers' Councils. Initially these Workers' Councils had mainly advisory functions and the key role of the director in running the enterprise was not infringed:

> A director shall organise the process of production as an enterprise and directly conduct the realisation of the plan and the operation of the enterprise, enforcing the laws and other prescriptions, the conclusions of the managing board of the enterprise and the orders and instructions of the appropriate state organs, as well as of the managing board and the director of the higher economic association.
>
> A director shall be directly responsible for the enforcement of the laws, or other legal prescriptions and the orders of the appropriate state organs, and he shall ensure their application in an enterprise. Within the economic plan and conforming to the conclusions of the managing board of an enterprise, the director . . . shall make contracts and allocate the working assets. A contract shall be valid as soon as made by the director. A director shall represent an enterprise before the state organs and in the legal relations with different physical and legal persons. He may authorise another person to represent the enterprise in determinate legal matters.
>
> The director of an enterprise shall hire workers and appoint other employees in the enterprise, except those concerning whom it was otherwise decreed by the special prescriptions, and he shall issue the decisions relating to their labour relations with the enterprise. The director . . . shall make decisions relating to the termination of

employment of the workers and office employees, unless this power was delegated to other persons in the enterprise on the basis of general prescriptions.[2]

Hence in the early 1950s the Worker's Councils were still subordinated to the managers, who in turn were responsible to the central economic ministries as economic planning was still dominated by the centre.

The distribution of income within enterprises was one of the key questions in the development of Workers' Councils. Originally, the board of managers — not the Workers' Council — made the first draft of income scales, although the latter could comment or object. The draft scale with these comments then went to the People's Committees of the Commune. This body played a major part in income distribution right from the beginning; it ensured that income distribution within an enterprise would not be the sole responsibility of the workers. The People's Committee of the Commune was made up of local representatives from all walks of life and was directly elected by all adult citizens, although the factory workers played a particularly important role. This People's Committee was to act as the local organ of state authority and as the 'organ of popular self-government in the communes...' (Art. 1); the duty of the committee was to 'safeguard the economic, social and cultural development of a commune'.[3]

Directors of enterprises were appointed by a People's Committee upon the recommendation of a commission, 50 per cent of whose members were elected by Workers' Councils. As Singleton points out, the changes of the early 1950s constituted the first step towards the decentralisation of economic decision-making. The Commune replaced the federal or republic government as the responsible body for the general direction of economic policy and was initially linked to the Workers' Councils which operated in its territory. The Commune's role was particularly important in the raising and distribution of funds for new enterprises. The financial allocation, after having been passed by the Workers' Councils, was examined by the financial and labour-planning department of the Commune and put before a full meeting of other producers' councils. The latter must

> carry out a general study [of the reports of the workers' councils] at the end of each half year ... and are entitled to make recommendations to the workers' councils concerning the distribution of the net income and other aspects of the economic management of the undertaking directly related to the targets of the national economic

plan, investment programmes, vocational training schemes, etc. ... The representatives of the workers' councils are also normally entitled to attend the sitting of the producers' council at which the position of the undertaking is discussed ... The workers' council ... must then meet once more and consider the recommendations of the producers' council.[4]

These considerable changes in the running of industry were accompanied by equally substantial changes in the political sphere. At the Sixth Party Congress in November 1952 the Communist Party changed its name to League of Communists, symbolising the government's intention to change the relationship between party and state. Now the position of the party was said to be that of an arbiter, without formal responsibility for running current affairs. The new policies were given a theoretical basis at the seventh congress in Ljublitana in 1958 where the 'bureaucratic-elitist form of socialism' was dismissed as a threat to the revolution. It was argued that the central forms of state management could play a positive role in the early stages of industrialisation to overcome backwardness. But once this early stage had been passed there was the danger that 'the state may turn into a factory of stagnation, into a fetter of social development'.[5] State and party apparatus may grow so strong that they 'might impose themselves as a force over and above society'. This explains the tendency towards direct democracy so that the state will begin to wither away. With the development of a socialist consciousness there will also be new forms of social and economic organisation. This will by no means be reached quickly. There will be a long evolutionary period during which the state still has to perform vital functions, but: 'It will be an instrument of force, and more and more an instrument of social self-government, based on the consciousness of the common material interests of working people and on the concrete needs of their producing organisations.'[6] The League of Communists will give the ideological guidance on this path. These changes did not challenge the leading role of the Communist League. While in subsequent years the role of the workers' councils was to become more and more important, there was never any doubt that the majority of vital posts in the new institutions were to continue to be held by members of the League.

The second step on the way to the 'four Ds' — decentralisation, de-etatisation, depoliticisation and democratisation[7] — was taken in the mid-1960s. After many discussions involving the whole nation, in April 1963 a new constitution was passed by the Federal Assembly and the

Socialist Alliance – the two legislative organs of the state. Eduard Kardelj, Yugoslav Prime Minister, had this to say when introducing the draft:

> [It] reflects the socialist order but does not conserve it ..., defends the achievements of the revolution, but simultaneously encourages the democratic evolution of society ... co-ordinates trends, but does not seek their uniformity ... The highest aim of the socialist state is finally to cease to be an instrument for the governing of people, and to become a joint organisational instrument to enable free people to manage things.[8]

The act of 1963 extended self-management from industry to all other areas of society such as education, culture, health and administrative bodies. The Federal Assembly was reconstructed. It now had five chambers, with 120 members each, and a Chamber of Nationalities with 70 members. The deputies to the Federal Chamber were elected by all citizens on the basis of territorial constituencies. Deputies to the remaining four chambers – the Economic Chamber, the Chamber of Education and Culture, the Chamber of Social Welfare and Health and the Political-Organisational Chamber – were elected on the basis of a limited and indirect franchise from special electorates representing various interest groups in whose name they were to act, e.g. Workers' Councils, public employees, teachers or doctors. The Chamber of Nationalities was composed of ten representatives of the republican assemblies of each of the six republics and five each from the assemblies of the two autonomous provinces.[9] The principle of rotation was applied to all elected offices, excluding President Tito who, because of his services to the nation, was to remain President until his death. Moreover it was forbidden for any individual, except Tito, to hold high offices simultaneously in the government and in the League of Communists. This made the Yugoslav system more liberal than those of its socialist neighbours.

The system of Workers' Councils and self-management did not free Yugoslavia from the problem of moving from an extensive to an intensive economy. By the mid-1960s the Yugoslav planners were thinking out new formulas. Although on the sheer macro level, Yugoslav production was enormous (though no higher than in the other socialist countries), there was a considerable need to improve the micro level of quality and precision. Not surprisingly they looked for the answer in the direction of further decentralisation. Efficiency was to be achieved

Yugoslavia: Communist League and Workers' Councils

through the 'discipline of the market'. Autonomous enterprises, within the system of workers' self-management, were to compete with each other and also on the world market. There was to be little central control.

The new reforms were introduced in 1965. Above all the role of the banks was changed in that they were given additional funds so that enterprise could borrow for investments.[10] Also a more flexible price policy was adopted and the worker-run enterprises would now determine the distribution of enterprise revenues, including their own wages. In 1971 a third and so far final series of decentralisation measures was introduced. Workers' Councils were given greater powers in the decision-making process in respect of the allocation of surplus funds among personal income, investment, social welfare funds and other purposes. Previously, they were limited in their powers over investment to 'expanded reproduction'.[11] To avoid the emergence of a capital market, the new law demanded that if an enterprise invested money in a bank, the bank had to return the profit it made to the investor. There was also a clause in the 1971 act which guaranteed the right to work with their own 'means of production' and to employ workers on a contracted basis.

There is still a considerable private sector in Yugoslavia. Above all 80 per cent of agriculture is still run privately but also in the catering, craft and service industries (such as road haulage and others), the private enterprise system prevails. These then, briefly summarised, are the main points of the Yugoslav self-management system. As Josef Wilczynski correctly depicts, this should not be seen as a path towards capitalism.

> Contrary to many enthusiastic expectations in the West, there is no evidence of these countries returning to Capitalism, not even in Yugoslavia. The Marxian ideal of Full Communism is still the declared ultimate goal of Socialist development, and outside observers can easily mistake means for ends. Many new elements incorporated into the Socialist economies, such as profit, economic incentives to labour, interest, flexible prices, independence of enterprises, are not identical with those operating under Capitalism as they are conditioned in different ways. The limitations of the market are recognized not only in Socialist countries but also in the Capitalist world. The market is not the best mechanism to shape structural developments, new production capacities and progress in science and technology in accordance with long-run social preferences.[12]

Compared to the Hungarian model, the role of market forces is much greater and the role of planning is less. The principle of workers' self-management differs from policies pursued in Hungary, and the incomes of workers depend much more on the financial results of their enterprise than is the case in Hungary and elsewhere in the socialist countries. Foreign trade policy is also more liberalised than Hungary's. Alec Nove, in his short but valuable examination of the Yugoslav model, tries to weigh what could be ranked as its advantages and disadvantages. The principle advantage, as is of course strongly stressed by the regime's ideologues, is the sense of participation. The Yugoslav interpretation of Karl Marx rejects overt centralised planning because of its threat of bureaucratisation and alienation of the workers. This necessitates the market because without such a mechanism there would have to be central planning to assess needs and issue instructions, and so a return to Soviet-style centralisation. This would be incompatible with workers' self-management.[13]

Yet these arguments have been attacked. Critics point to an overemphasis on micro-profitability and free market fanaticism which is not always in line with the commonwealth.[14] In fact, one economic historian even claims that the Yugoslav economy is run along an Adam Smithian line to an extent that is quite uncommon for Europe as a whole. Nove also points to profitability and income distribution:

> The principle of workers' self-management contains a flaw. If the income of the workers is not significantly affected by the net revenues of the enterprise, then they have little material interest in the outcome. If, on the other hand, the successful enterprise pays much more to its workers than a less successful one, the material interest is indeed present, but the differential is bound to be resented, as it offends a widely held sense of fairness. Why should a worker who does his job well receive much less than another of equal skill and application, but whose enterprise happens to be profitable? This may, almost certainly will, be due to circumstances over which any individual worker has no control, and in reality the role in management of a rank-and-file worker cannot be significant. Equal pay for equal work is a principle which extends not only to pay rates as between men and women. In practice, knowledge that other workers in successful enterprises earn more is a cause of pressure for higher distribution of income to the workers elsewhere, and this constitutes an important source of inflationary pressure. The evidence clearly shows that the Yugoslav system is more inflation-

prone than the Hungarian, and the powers of worker-elected councils over the apportionment of enterprise net income is surely one reason for this.[15]

Following on from this Nove also doubts whether the rank and file 'participates' as much as is claimed and he refers to the left-wing critics who stress the undesirable spread of commercialism, consumerism, advertising, income differentials (workers are willing to pay good managers well; they are not so egalitarian as left-wing intellectuals). They are unhappy with the market as a basis for any sort of socialism because 'the workers cannot really dominate the use of their means of production, because their use is in fact dominated by market relations'.[16]

If the Yugoslav model was principally adopted out of fear of bureaucratisation, then there is so far little evidence from Yugoslavia's own critics that it has been overcome. Nor does the optimism about income policies, which is advanced by the theoreticians, seem to match the reality. It was argued that responsibility and decision-making power would curb the desire of the workforce to give themselves excessive wage rises.

> Working collectives aim towards a permanent rise in the standards of living. As this is the real stimulus for the working people to associate in collectives of commodity producers — and as this aim cannot be realised without extending production — it will be obvious that it is in the subjective interest of the working collectives to ensure conditions for a permanent rise in the standards of living, i.e., a permanent increase in consumption, by allocating a part of the earned income for capital formation (in order to extend production). If the total current income is used for personal consumption, the collectives would not be able to extend production, which in turn is the only way of ensuring a permanent increase in personal income. This leads us to conclude that it is in the interest of the working collectives to allocate a part of the earned revenue for capital formation . . . and to use only the remaining part of the income for their current personal consumption.[17]

As Singleton points out, arguments are sound convincing to academic economists may be looked at in a different light by the shopfloor worker when he comes to cast his vote in favour of either jam today or a pie in the sky. Between 1965 and 1970, for example, the cost of living index rose by an average of 10 per cent while incomes rose at twice this rate, which does indicate that the workers were very generous with their wage policy. This obviously adds to inflationary pressures.

The traditional ethnic and geographic problems have not been overcome. The country of the 'South Slavs' was a constant trouble spot in the years leading up to the First World War. In the kingdom of Yugoslavia, which emerged after the First World War, the conflict between the national groups — especially between the Serbs and Croats — was, together with economic and political backwardness, one of many factors which prevented the newly-founded state from functioning properly. In the post-war period, the nationality problem did not reach such massive proportions but it lingered on and few would claim today that it has been solved. Basically the problem is economic. Yugoslavia today is made up of eight republics and provinces: Serbia, Slovenia, Croatia, Vojvodina, Kosovo, Bosnia, Montenegro and Macedonia.[18] The first four have reached a relatively advanced state of industrial development. The other four, having had to start from a position of extreme backwardness, have found it hard to reach the level of their more prosperous neighbours. Income discrepancies between the most affluent republic (Slovenia) and the poorest (Kosovo) amount to 5 to 1, which is a hefty margin. Naturally the poorer parts expect to have additional funds invested in their region so they can catch up. Not unexpectedly also, the 'haves' object to their resources being so diverted. The Croations in particular strongly voiced their discontent and in November and December 1971 it came to an outbreak of open unrest at Zagreb. It was claimed, for example, that in 1971, 30 per cent of Croatia's national income was being transferred to other republics. The Croatians also objected to the steady drain of their workers abroad. Some nationalist writers implied that Croatia's best young men were being forced to leave their motherland because there was no economic future at home. On the other hand, Croatia is not only 'putting into the system'. The Croatian tourist industry, which nets several hundred million dollars per year, was only made possible by large federal investment to build highways, hotels and transport facilities. The north-south trade within Yugoslavia also worked clearly to the advantage of Croatia. Another factor of complaint in the Yugoslav federation is the predominant position of the Serbs in both party and the government. The Serbs, the largest group with 40 per cent of the total population, are said to be disproportionally represented in key offices.

These problems do not seem insoluble. The Yugoslav agrarian crisis is more serious. Yugoslavia, not unlike Poland, retained a predominantly small-holder agriculture. Some 80 per cent of Yugoslavia's agriculture is made up of small private holdings and, with no specific policy for modernisation either along Western lines or along the model of the Eastern co-operatives, the crisis in Yugoslavia's agriculture has reached 'Polish proportions'. Low yields, an ageing rural population and the flight to the city are familiar phenomena. The impact of the poor state of agriculture is not as drastic here because, unlike Poland, Yugoslavia so far has had more means to counter-balance badly functioning elements of the economy. No doubt because of Poland's brave anti-Soviet policies, Western aid has been provided from the 1950s on a lavish scale. The hope of the Yugoslav federation to achieve a favourable trade balance never materialised but luckily the Yugoslavs could reduce this gap by their pro-Western policies. The US lent 20 million dollars to the dissident Soviet ally in 1949 and during the 1950s United States aid to Yugoslavia was greater than that given to India and only surpassed by that provided for Greece and Turkey.

The successful tourist boom of the 1960s paid impressive dividends on the investment in tourism (see Tables 9.1 and 9.2).[19]

Table 9.1: Foreign Tourists and their Overnight Stays, 1953-71 (thousands)

	Tourist	Overnight stays
1953	245	855
1954	321	1,104
1955	485	1,833
1956	394	1,333
1957	499	1,966
1958	598	2,509
1959	835	3,433
1960	873	3,511
1961	1,080	4,523
1962	1,242	5,270
1963	1,755	7,650
1964	2,272	10,085
1965	2,658	11,240
1966	3,437	14,720
1967	3,678	16,107
1968	3,887	17,210
1969	4,836	22,400
1970	4,748	22,560
1971	5,260	25,873

Table 9.2: Income from Tourism: (in $US million)

1965	1966	1968	1969	1970	1971	1972	1973
81	116	182	241	274	360	432	595

Finally, the decision to let people work in the West added to the influx of Western valuta. As many as one million workers were said to work mainly in the German Federal Republic in the 1960s and 1970s. Table 9.3 gives the value of their remittances.[20]

Table 9.3: Remittances of Migrants (in $US)

1965	1966	1968	1969	1970	1971	1972	1973
59	95	122	206	500	650	870	1,209

As Tables 9.2 and 9.3 show, invisible earnings in 1973 were approaching the 2 billion dollar mark. The problem with this huge influx of Western money is that it rests on a very shallow basis. By the mid-1970s Yugoslavia had to compete with other mass tourist centres all around the world for the British and German market and this competition is tough. Not surprisingly, there were strong signs of alarm and soul-searching when the tourist trade declined in the mid-1970s. The Yugoslav tourist services had to realise that the standards they were offering were deteriorating and that they needed to improve facilities if they wanted to remain competitive. For the domestic tourist it had become cheaper to go to Greece than to choose a Yugoslav tourist resort.

The income from workers abroad, especially from West Germany, also has its flaws. As the Western economies are now struggling, they might reverse their open-door policy and some might even ask their *Gastarbeiter* (guest-workers) to leave. The West German CSU leader Franz Josef Strauss, the candidate for the position of chancellor in 1980, did advocate such a step and should the Federal Republic's economy continue to deteriorate such a solution may be adopted.

But above all, invisible income does not help with the two major shortcomings of the Yugoslav model, inflation and unemployment. The other socialist countries take legitimate pride in keeping both under control as far as possible. Unemployment in particular is ideologically totally unacceptable, as the right to work is a basic right and a necessary condition for the socialist concept of freedom to be realised.[21] Inflation, as has been mentioned, has always been a problem. In addition to the factors already listed, there is a tendency to over-investment:

> The problem here is ultimate responsibility. If an enterprise wishes to expand, by borrowing from the bank, it puts up a good case for future profitability. Suppose, however, there is a loss. Who is to suffer? The manager may by then have moved elsewhere. The workers' council collectively cannot be financially punished, though in extreme cases it can be dissolved and a temporary manager appointed from above, as a consequence of insolvency – the nearest approach to bankruptcy. The rate of interest charged and the obligation to repay the loan are insufficient restraints on the demand for capital. Lack of central control can also easily lead to duplication of investments, with loss of potential economies of scale. All this is consistent with a high growth rate, which Yugoslavia has indeed achieved. But it is a further spur to inflation.[22]

The Yugoslav labour-managed enterprises are so set on maximising the net product per employee that they are not interested in taking on additional employees as would a Soviet-type enterprise or, indeed, even a capitalist one under conditions in which unemployment is a major problem. Unemployment is alleged to amount to several hundred thousand, a figure which would be worse were it not for the guest-workers in Germany.

We have already referred to the 5 to 1 income discrepancy between regions. There are also discrepancies among groups in the community. Bureaucrats and skilled workers take the cream, the unemployed and others fall short. The fact that people in key positions are better placed for getting consumer goods and other luxuries is a problem in all socialist countries and is of course greatly resented by the less privileged sections of the community. It seems more strongly pronounced in Yugoslavia than elsewhere. This may also explain why notwithstanding the relative affluence of some, overall living standards are below most other East European states (see Table 9.4).[23]

Not surprisingly, this had led to demands from 'Eastern-orientated' sections of the League to return to a more centrally-based policy. They are backed by intellectuals who are severely critical of the inequalities which have emerged under the present system. The strong trade links with the West rule out a major step in this direction. But there are many clouds in the sky of post-Tito Yugoslavia.

Table 9.4: Per Capita Income of CMEA Countries and Yugoslavia in US Dollars in 1976

GDR	4.000
CSSR	3.600
Poland	3.500
USSR	3.400
Hungary	3.300
Bulgaria	2.700
Romania	2.600
Yugoslavia	1.450

Notes and References

1. For details Fred Singleton, *Twentieth Century Yugoslavia* (Macmillan London, 1976), pp. 124 ff.
2. Ibid., pp. 127-8.
3. Ibid., p. 129.
4. Ibid., p. 131.
5. Ibid., p. 135.
6. Ibid.
7. R. Bicanic, in *Foreign Affairs*, no. 44 (1966) quoted in Singleton, *Twentieth Century Yugoslavia*, p. 138.
8. Singleton, ibid., pp. 144-5.
9. Singleton, ibid., p. 146.
10. For details, ibid., pp. 269-72.
11. Ibid.
12. Wilczynski, *Socialist Economic Development*, p. 59.
13. Nove, *Soviet Economic System*, p. 300.
14. Nove points out that at their worst, Yugoslav free-market fanatics even required that a research institute in the chemical industry be profitable and asks the question: does the research division of Imperial Chemical Industries make a profit as such? He also points to the greatly confused railway administration, caused by the separate profit-oriented operation of each republic's rail network.
15. Ibid., pp. 300-1.
16. Ibid., p. 302; in Nove's view this contains a fundamental weakness of the entire 'new left' position. He asks what then is to determine the activities of the producers, as production is ultimately for use. If they do not distribute goods through the market then there is only the 'plan' alternative and that is what the Yugoslav model tried to get away from.
17. Singleton, *Twentieth Century Yugoslavia*, pp. 162-3.
18. Ibid., p. 221.
19. Ibid., pp. 182, 181.
20. Ibid.
21. See Chapter 4 on Hungary.
22. Nove, *Soviet Economic System*, p. 301.
23. J. Wilczynski, 'How they live in Comecon', *Current Affairs Bulletin*, vol. 57, no. 3 (August 1980), pp. 4-16.

10 TOWARDS A CONSUMER SOCIETY

The visitor to Eastern Europe today will quickly note that consumerism has arrived. Although the range of goods on offer is still well behind Western countries, the days of austerity have passed. The reasons for the slow start towards a more consumer-orientated society are obvious. Consumerism was part of capitalist society — it highlighted its inequalities. It was said to encourage acquisitiveness, an element alien to a socialist society, and to deprive life of its human content. It was also said that consumerism was conducive to waste and caused under-utilisation. On a more practical level, priority had to be given to the development of a sound industrial basis to produce goods considered more urgently in demand. Hence the continuously high level of investment industry. To achieve the basic prerequisites for a socialist society — free health care for everyone, education, culture, job security — heavy strains were placed on the gross national product. It was not until a solid foundation was laid that more attention was given to consumerism, and the stage reached today could be described as a 'liberal form of consumer free choice'.[1] On the one hand, overall consumption and broad structures are laid down by the centre plan and so are long-term investment programmes for major developments in the consumer goods industries. On the other hand, the composition and distribution of the output in the consumer goods sector are determined by individual consumers registering their preference in the market.[2]

The symbol of consumer society in the twentieth century is the private motor car, which arrived very late in the socialist countries. As J. Wilczynski points out that there were ideological objections. The institution of private ownership would mean capitulation to the acquisitive instinct of egoistic man, amounting to the transplantation of capitalism onto socialist soil. Also, it would introduce a visible symbol of social distinction, as some people would be able to acquire better cars than others owing to their higher earning or saving capacity, while many others would not be able to afford them at all. Moreover, it would encourage anti-social individualism, as the private car largely removes people from public transport and various social pursuits. As such, the private car is contrary to communist conscience and is not conducive to the evolution of the ideal 'New Communist Man'.[3] Even stronger were the economic arguments. With the partial exception of the GDR and Czechoslovakia, all the socialist countries started from a backward and poor position and could not afford the luxury of an automobile industry. Car production is highly capital intensive and requires not only costly auxiliary enterprises such as the metal, electric, glass and rubber parts industries but also road-building and other services needed by motorists. In the early years there were more important fields to concentrate upon. Up to the mid-1960s, automobile production was geared not for consumer demand but for official usage. In 1960, in the region of the nine European socialist countries, 280,000 passenger cars were produced, less than in Canada that year. Thus, these countries (including the Soviet Union), with 15 per cent of world population, 29 per cent of world industrial output and 18 per cent of the world's area, contributed only 2 per cent of the world's output of motor cars. The importance given to 'productive purpose' is seen in the fact that in 1960 427,000 trucks were manufactured, compared with only 280,000 motor cars.[4]

During the 1960s this changed. The first wave of basic industrialisation had by then been completed and consumer goods were given a higher priority. At the same time, consumer expectation added pressure to the demand for privately owned motor cars. From the mid-1960s car production sky-rocketed in Eastern Europe, increasing twenty-two-fold from 96,000 to 2,130,000 in the period from 1956 to 1977. In the capitalist world, it rose only threefold. The overall share of the socialist countries in the world's output of cars rose from 1 to 7 per cent (see Table 10.1).[5]

Table 10.1: The Growth of the Passenger Car Output in the Socialist and Leading Capitalist Countries, 1950-77

Country	1950	1960	1970	1975	1976	1977
USSR	64	139	344	1,201	1,239	1,250
Poland	—	13	65	174	229	280
Yugoslavia	—	9	63	130	139	180
GDR	7	64	127	159	164	169
Czechoslovakia	25	56	143	175	179	158
Romania	—	1	24	68	71	73
Bulgaria	—	—	—	12	15	20
European socialist countries	96	282	766	1,919	2,036	2,130
% of world output	1.1	2.2	3.4	7.7	7.0	7.8

Towards a Consumer Society

Today there are 17 major types of passenger cars and as most of the makes are manufactured in several models, the total number of models produced at present is about 80. There is a great deal of co-operation in automobile production among the CMEA countries. Many types of cars are produced in more than one country, and in recent years there have also been long-term production agreements with Citroen, Fiat, Renault, Volkswagen, Daimler Benz and Volvo.

As Table 10.2 shows, East European motor car production is still well behind the West, as is car distribution per thousand.[6]

Table 10.2: Passenger Cars in Use per 1,000 of Population in the European Comecon and Selected Other Countries, 1960-76

Country	1960	1970	1976
Bulgaria	–	14	25
Czechoslovakia	20	57	112
GDR	17	67	122
Hungary	3	24	60
Poland	4	15	38
Romania	–	6	10
USSR	–	7	20
Australia[a]	197	311	388
Canada[a]	229	308	443
West Germany	81	219	310
Greece	5	25	53
India[a]	1	1	1
Indonesia	1	2	3
Japan	5	85	168
USA	340	434	528
Yugoslavia	3	35	73
WORLD[b]	33	53	66

(a) Including vehicles operated by police and other government authorities.
(b) Without China, North Korea and Vietnam.
– Not available.

There is obviously still a considerable gap, although the leading nations of the socialist countries are catching up and the USSR has now become the world's seventh largest producer of motor cars. The price of cars is also much higher than in the West and there are waiting lists of several years. Jozef Wilczynski believes that the socialist countries, having observed the many difficulties caused by full-scale motorisation in the West, will put a ceiling on ownership at 200 per 1,000 or two families in three. This would create a substantial under-privileged minority which would be hard to defend on ideological grounds. Hence, unless the drying up of the world's oil resources will put an end to the car as we know it today, the age of the motor car should have reached all of Eastern Europe by the end of the century.

As far as household items are concerned, the situation had improved by the mid-1970s. Radios, black and white televisions, washing machines and refrigerators are widely available as Table 10.3 indicates.[7] Colour television sets are still rare and high quality stereo and hi-fi equipment are out of the reach of most people. Furniture and clothes are available, although most items come on to the market very sporadically and queueing is still a familiar feature. The irregularity in the supply of many consumer durables and the modest quality of many goods is irritating for the customer, and to speak of a 'consumer revolution'[8] is too optimistic even for the GDR. The relatively poor supply of consumer goods is a sore point for the European socialist countries. It affects people's everyday lives and experience has shown that it is dangerous to make too many demands upon the population. The socialist countries devote only between 60-65 per cent of the gross national product to current consumption compared to 75-90 per cent in the West. Few would argue that the state of the *Wegwerfgesellschaft* ('Throw-away society'), which the most affluent Western nations are privileged to enjoy, is a desirable target to reach. Yet when it is difficult for a customer to walk into a leading East Berlin store at any time and be able to purchase a pair of underpants in the correct size, it is not an acceptable state of affairs.

Table 10.3: Consumer Durables in Selected Comecon Countries in 1960 and 1976 (number per 100 households)

Country	Year	Radios	TV	Washing machines	Refrigerators	Vacuum cleaners
Czechoslovakia	1960	89	21	54	11	—
	1976	176	96	115	83	60
GDR	1960	90	17	6	6	—
	1976	97	84	76	90	25
Hungary	1960	72	3	15	1	4
	1972	75	61	61	46	37
Poland	1960	177	14	—	—	—
	1976	129	95	93	77	71
USSR	1960	46	8	4	4	3
	1976	81	77	67	67	20

Towards a Consumer Society

Whilst consumer production is still a weak spot, the strength of the Eastern European system hitherto lay in the fields of social security and social services. Job security and full employment are valuable assets and income has risen steadily.

Table 10.4: Per Capita National Income in the Comecon and Selected Other Countries in 1976 (at market prices in US dollars)[a]

Comecon countries		Selected other countries	
	(This axis is not to scale)		
		− 8,330	Switzerland
		− 8,030	Sweden
		− 6,970	USA
		− 6,710	Australia
		− 6,470	West Germany
		− 5,870	France
		− 4,290	Japan
GDR	4,000 −		
		− 3,860	New Zealand
Czechoslovakia	3,600 −		
		− 3,550	United Kingdom
Poland	3,500 −		
USSR	3,400 −		
Hungary	3,300 −		
		− 2,720	Italy
Bulgaria	2,700 −		
Romania	2,600 −		
		− 2,350	Greece
		− 1,500	Portugal
		− 1,450	Yugoslavia
		− 1,390	Brazil
Mongolia	1,200 −		
		− 1,140	Mexico
Cuba	1,100 −		
		− 1,070	South Africa
		− 680	Chile
		− 400	China (PR of)
		− 240	Indonesia
		− 150	Uganda
		− 130	India
		− 100	Bangladesh
		− 80	Vietnam
WORLD AVERAGE 1,400 WORLD AVERAGE			

(a) The Western concept of national income is used throughout. The figures are rounded, to avoid a misleading impression of the possibility of precise measurement.

As Table 10.4 shows, the GDR has now surpassed Great Britain in per capita national income.[9] Most socialist countries still rank below the rich Western nations but they have moved above those Western countries like Spain, Greece and even Italy which started from a similar position of economic backwardness in 1945. While income has risen, prices have remained comparatively steady. According to a United Nation's source, in the period 1970-7 the consumer price index remained unchanged in the GDR. Prices rose by 3 per cent in the CSSR, 24 per cent in Poland and 25 per cent in Hungary. By contrast, they rose by 108 per cent in Australia, 56 per cent in the United States and 46 per cent in the Federal Republic of Germany.[10] Since then, these differences would have further increased in favour of the socialist nations.

Social services are given high priority. All CMEA countries are noted for a very well-developed and comprehensive system of social services provided by the state directly or by specialised institutions such as the trade unions or the social welfare branches of enterprises. Most social benefits are provided on a contributory basis and may be in cash or services. These include social security against blindness, deafness and other incapacities; free to all are hospital, medical and dental services and education at all levels. Medicine, glasses, hearing aids, dentures, milk to nursing mothers and children, school books, theatre tickets, housing and some basic foodstuffs are subsidised by the state. Old age pensions are adequate and in some countries very generous. The retirement age for men ranges from 60 in Bulgaria, CSSR, Hungary and Romania to 65 in the GDR and Poland and for women from 55 to 60 respectively.[11] In arduous occupations the retiring age is lower. A further achievement of the socialist welfare state is the generous provision of various forms of recreational facilities by enterprises or the unions.

The GDR's social policies probably lead Europe today. We have referred already to the high priorities given to creches and kindergartens and to its advanced education standards. Paid pregnancy leave in the GDR is 18 weeks and on birth the mother is given a grant of 1,000 marks (more than an average monthly income) and is entitled to a year's leave on full pay. Housing is cheap, running at approximately 5 per cent of income, but the housing shortage will not be overcome for at least another decade. Nor has the mass construction of flats brought architectural masterpieces, although the creation of parks and other recreation areas should eventually give a more pleasant image to some of the huge new settlement centres such as Berlin-Marzahn. The

GDR authorities fully realise that neglect of housing policies leads to over-crowding, tensions and high divorce rates.

The position of women compares favourable to the West. In 1972 the GDR introduced one of the most liberal abortion laws and at the same time made the pill available free of charge: Steele sums it up well:

> The old German principle that the woman should attend to the three Ks — *Kinder, Kirche, Küche* (children, church and kitchen) — is dead. In the early post-war years many women may have gone out to work mainly to increase the family's income. Over the years attitudes have changed. The vast majority of women in the GDR work because they want the satisfaction of a job outside the home. In 1960 two out of every three women of working age had jobs. By 1973 it was 84 percent. Put another way, nearly half the total workforce were women (whereas in West Germany they formed only 37 percent of the workforce in 1971). Women frequently do jobs which in Britain and the United States are almost invariably done by men. They drive buses and cranes. They are judges and surgeons. On a collective farm near the Polish frontier I saw two huge combine harvesters in the same field, one driven by a man, the other by his wife. Increasingly East German women expect and are getting opportunities for promotion on a level with men. There are still problems. The party leader Erich Honecker has admitted that it is easier to decree equality than implement it. 'It is one of the great achievements of socialism', he said, 'to have brought about the equality of women in our state both legally and to a great extent in practice'.

Women are most nearly on a par with men in the judiciary. In 1973 45 percent of lay judges were women, and 36 percent were professional judges. Among trade union officials 44 percent were women. In local government and the People's Chamber roughly one out of every three deputies is a woman. Women are less well represented at the top. Although they provided almost half the party's membership, only one woman, Inge Lange, is among the twenty-three members and candidate member of the Politbüro. The Minister for Education Dr Margot Honecker, wife of the party secretary, is the only female member of the Government. Roughly 60 percent of the country's teachers are women, but they fill only a quarter of the headships in schools. These statistics show that full equality is some way off. However, they are still on a rising trend, and are better than most countries in the West. They probably reflect not so much continuing discrimination as the fact that women have so far had a harder time getting further education and specialisation. In 1967 the Government brought in special courses for working women, and a scheme whereby factories will supplement a woman's scholarship by up to 80 percent of her previous net salary while she studies.[12]

But as Steele points out, old habits die hard. Women come home from work as tired as the man, but then have to take the major responsibility for shopping, cooking, cleaning and the laundry. According to a survey published in 1968 women spent an average of 47.6 hours a week on housework while men spent about 7 hours. The full breakdown of the division of labour was as shown in Table 10.5.[13]

Table 10.5: The Division of Household Labour

Type of work	Wife	Husband	Miscellaneous[a]
		in % of time	
Meal preparation	84.2	6.8	12.0
House cleaning	78.8	12.5	9.0
Laundry	89.7	2.9	7.4
Shopping	76.5	11.8	11.7

(a) 'Miscellaneous' is work performed by some other person.

The position in the other socialist countries is not so favourable and 'old habits' are indeed dying slowly. No one would make the absurd claim that equality has been achieved — it would have needed more than a miracle to do so within a generation and a half. However, it would be even more absurd to claim, as was done in a recent American sociological survey, that the 'truly revolutionary legislation and party politics towards women' which were introduced soon after the establishment of socialism did not lead to changes in the role of the women. The author, Barbara Jancar, sees the main reason for this alleged shortcoming 'in the inherent authoritarian position characteristic in communist society'. She claims that because of the ideological narrowness of communist governments they have taken up an increasingly conservative stand. This is illustrated by the fact that women in socialist society are predominantly found in the 'caring and curing' professions — in which they have always worked — such as education, medicine, book-keeping, food and textile industry and more recently chemistry and biology.[14] The listing of medicine among traditional women's jobs is a surprise inclusion from an Anglo-Saxon author because in all Anglo-Saxon countries Medical Practitioners' Associations have been and still are the backbone of conservative male dominance. The GDR figures show that women are breaking into professions that were previously male-dominated to a greater extent than is the case in Western countries. Indeed, if anything, the material presented in Jancas's study confirms rather than undermines that this is also the case in other socialist countries.

Recent events in Poland should not blur the fact that constitutionally much has been achieved since the days of Stalin. Although the notion of the 'proletarian dictatorship' forms a part of Marxist ideology, it has given way to the far more liberal concept of 'all sections of the community under the leadership of the party'. And although elections in Eastern Europe differ from Western-style elections, the composition of most representative institutions — from local councils to national legislative chambers — shows a far wider range of citizens from all walks of life participating than is the case in the West. The concept of people's democracies is not a mere façade even if the decisions on the key policy issues are undertaken at the level of the party leadership. But this is scarcely different from the West.

How then does the socialist East and the West compare? Writing in 1970 Jozef Wilczynski tried to list the advantages and disadvantages. Wilczynski lists eight advantages which, in his opinion, socialism enjoys over capitalism. First, there is the mainspring of economic activities. Production processes are not determined by a 'whimsical market mechanism' resting on private profit motive but by an economic plan which expresses the need for society as a whole. Appeal, Wilczynski points out, is made to higher social instincts and profit is treated merely as a means rather than an end. The market is harnessed within the framework of planning and so it becomes a useful instrument, a servant instead of a master. Secondly, there is the level of employment. The social ownership of the means of production and central economic planning enables the maintenance of continuous full employment. A socialist economy is not prone to overproduction and cyclical fluctuations. Where unemployment and fluctuations have occurred, as in Yugoslavia, they were caused by excessive reliance on market mechanisms. Thirdly, the rate of growth is higher in the socialist world. Between 1950 and 1970 the average annual growth rate of the national income in the European socialist countries was 8 per cent as compared to 5 per cent in the West and that of industrial output was 10 per cent and 5 per cent respectively. Moreover these countries' share in the world's industrial output increased from less than 10 per cent in 1938 to about 30 per cent in 1970, and reached 37 per cent by 1980. In the leading Western nations, basic industrialisation took some 25 to 50 years to achieve, but in the European socialist countries this process was completed in 12 to 20 years. In view of the semi-feudal conditions inherited, the absence of colonies, the widespread wartime devastation, Western boycotts and the strategic embargo, and with practically no aid from the capitalist world, their achievements can be described by objective observers as spectacular.[15]

Finally, Wilczynski refers to the 'dignity of labour'. By this he means that the social ownership of the means of production involves no fundamental cleavage between the employer and employees — no feeling of exploitation, no fear of unemployment, no disruptive strikes. The other four factors listed are the distribution of national income (more equal and less subject to exploitation), social-cost-benefits, prevention of certain forms of waste and a greater overall vitality.[16]

On the negative side Wilczynski lists an undue ideological and political dominance of the economic scene, a 'system . . . bedevilled with bureaucracy and inflexibility' and 'poor correspondence of decision-making between macro and micro levels'. The system is also said to be liable to errors being committed on a large scale, and it seems to be very difficult so far to devise a rational and workable pricing system. Finally Wilczynski also points to the insufficient incentive for competition, neglect of current consumption and limited personal freedom.[17] Against this one could reply that the comparatively short time since the system's inception and the extremely difficult circumstances under which it has operated should not be overlooked. Nor are the shortcomings and mistakes listed by Wilczynski insuperable: ways may be found to correct and modify them. Hence the gains outweigh the disadvantages. Some of Wilczynski's final points — for example, constraint of personal freedom and low efficiency — have not been borne out by the course of events in the 1970s and 1980s, which saw a trend towards more freedom in most countries. The economic crisis of the capitalist world of recent years has not hit the socialist countries as hard.

A further interesting study was made by a West German research team in 1972. They selected two countries, Greece and Bulgaria, which in terms of geography, size of population, state of economic development (mainly agrarian) before the Second World War and general history were very similar (both belonged to the Ottoman empire until the nineteenth century). Since the Second World War, Greece has

Towards a Consumer Society 149

remained in the capitalist orbit, while Bulgaria has become part of the socialist world. The survey was conducted among 500 families in both countries. The researchers made the initial comment that whilst they were free to conduct their survey they found in Greece almost without exception a certain overall restraint often mixed with fear which they did not at all observe in Bulgaria. This obviously was explained by the fact that Greece at that time was still run by the 'government of the colonels'. They did not regard this as a serious setback but felt that it might have slightly upgraded the positive component of the Greece figures. Altogether they asked 18 questions concerning people's everyday life. Many of their findings were interesting and surprising. Asked whether they expected for the coming year 'considerable economic growth' and 'considerable rise in the standard of living', 99 and 94 per cent respectively answered this question in the affirmative in Bulgaria. The corresponding figures in Greece were 77 and 76.[18] Asked whether they would expect 'considerable unemployment' and a 'disadvantageous inflation' the Bulgarians answered both questions with a 100 per cent 'no'. In the Greek survey, 89 per cent felt that they had no worry about unemployment but only 26 per cent felt that the inflation rate would not disadvantage them. The discrepancy between the two sets of figures has probably increased since the early 1970s.

Apel's study devotes a considerable section to 'quality of life'. It uses modern sociological measuring techniques which rely upon a scale of 1 to 5 (1 = very good, 2 = good, 3 = neither good nor bad, 4 = not satisfactory, 5 = bad). Hence a lower figure indicates higher satisfaction. Table 10.6 gives some of his findings.

Table 10.6: Quality of Life

	Bulgaria	Greece	Difference
Family life	1.68	1.82	0.14
Working climate	1.80	2.25	0.45
Health	2.00	2.06	0.06
Schooling	2.97	3.14	0.17
Housing	2.04	2.64	0.60
Financial situation	2.47	3.16	0.69
Social security	1.47	3.22	1.48
Evaluation of life as a whole	2.05	2.69	0.64

The authors point out that as far as 'family life' is concerned the woman in Greece still holds the traditional role as mother, housewife and sexual companion to her husband, who feels more at home with his friends in the coffee house than in his domestic situation. The claim often made in the West that the worker in Eastern Europe, deprived through the absence of 'free unions', feels exploited or carelessly treated is not borne out by the figures for 'working climate'. Apel claims that the health figures are over-rated in the Greek study, for average life expectancy in Greece is two years lower than in Bulgaria. The difference in levels of schooling is also more pronounced than the study indicates. Illiteracy in Greece is still 14 per cent compared to only 3 per cent in Bulgaria. The average number of years at school are 7.3 and 9.1 respectively. Of those entering school in Bulgaria, 64 per cent acquire a tertiary qualification, whereas the corresponding figure for Greece is only 15 per cent.[20] The differences in 'financial situation' and 'quality of life' are considerable but the biggest discrepancy is obviously in the social security bracket. The greater detail in Table 10.7 on 'social security' needs few comments (A refers to cities, B to towns and C to rural areas; D is the total).[21] That means the proportion of 1 and 2 to 3 and 4 is 88 per cent to 1 per cent in Bulgaria but 31 per cent to 44 per cent in Greece. As far as 'evaluation of life as a whole' is concerned, the relation is 63 to 4 per cent in the Bulgarian case but 30 to 24 per cent in the Greek example. As the authors aptly remark, these discrepancies are extraordinary.

Table 10.7: Social Security

Scale	Bulgaria A	B	C	D	Greece A	B	C	D
1 – very good	46	34	35	38	9	8	6	8
2 – good	44	52	54	50	25	26	19	23
3 – medium	9	13	10	11	28	22	23	25
4 – bad	1	1	1	1	26	31	29	28
5 – very bad	0	0	0	0	12	13	23	16

As far as economic growth is concerned between 1952 and 1970 the growth rate in Bulgaria exceeded Greece's by one fifth. This was the more surprising as Greece was integrated into the flourishing Western market system, whereas Bulgaria had a far more difficult start in the Eastern system. Greece has had access to huge sums of hard currency, much of it in the form of outright aid, while Bulgaria received nothing. Like Yugoslavia, Greek guest-workers added to the influx of hard currency. By 1956, 300 million dollars had been sent to Greece from

Towards a Consumer Society 151

guest-workers or migrants, a figure which had trebled by 1970.[22] This enormous influx of capital (amounting to 24 per cent of total national income in 1970) could have been used at least in part for investment as a basis for a reliable economic growth rate. In fact it was largely used for consumption.

From this one would expect that the Greek consumer would have fared better than his or her Bulgarian neighbour. The casual Western observer, making a brief comparison of shop windows in Athens and Sofia, would only too readily arrive at such a conclusion. But on closer analysis the superficial impression is false. Personal income in Bulgaria for the years 1952 to 1970 was almost 50 per cent higher than in Greece and the income discrepancies between the top percentile earners and the bottom percentile is 2.5 in Bulgaria and 15 in Greece. Wealth is still much more pronounced in Greece but so is poverty. In 1972-3 the average income per month for the bottom 5 per cent of the income-earners was (US) $39 in Bulgaria and (US) $13 in Greece. Given the free provision of social services in the former country, even low income-earners are not poverty stricken in Bulgaria. The Greek figure reveals great hardship.

Table 10.8 for consumer durables and other household items shows that the lead in income for the Bulgarians is mirrored in the distribution of these goods and services.

Table 10.8: Selected Household Items[23]

| Household | \multicolumn{8}{c|}{Bulgaria} | \multicolumn{8}{c}{Greece} |
	I	II	III	IV	V	All	S	L	I	II	III	IV	V	All	S	L
Tap water	85	89	91	89	91	88	90	80	73	84	91	94	100	88	94	67
Warm water	49	48	60	65	65	56	59	42	28	38	45	62	84	51	61	13
Electricity	100	100	97	100	100	99	99	99	89	97	96	99	98	96	99	87
Electric washing machine	52	83	80	88	86	77	81	65	9	16	16	32	61	26	35	8
Electric refrigerator	45	72	70	72	79	67	68	66	43	63	70	81	91	70	82	45
Radio	85	98	95	95	99	94	95	93	75	86	86	97	99	89	92	79
Television	60	78	85	92	92	80	81	78	15	35	30	53	68	41	47	21
Bicycle	8	13	17	22	20	16	17	15	8	9	12	10	12	10	12	8
Motorbike	15	24	24	23	28	23	22	28	24	15	14	12	8	11	20	13
Car	7	14	12	24	29	17	20	13	7	11	12	26	48	21	23	15
Average	51	62	63	67	69	61	63	57	37	45	47	57	67	50	57	36
Greece's share of Bulgaria									73	73	75	85	96	82	90	63

Note: The Roman numeral refers to the income divided into five groups each comprising 20 per cent.

All this data enabled the authors to arrive at some conclusions and make some suggestions. Amongst other points, they claimed that the overall economic success, measured in terms of economic growth, was considerably higher in Bulgaria. So was the case with personal income. Income inequality is much higher in Greece and the difference in living standards between city and country is also much more pronounced there. The writers also felt that ability to speak up freely — although in theory more restricted in Bulgaria — was in practice more widespread than in Greece. From this the authors conclude that not all Western interpretations of developments in Eastern Europe are necessarily plausible. In particular there is no reason to believe that the neglect of consumer production is an insurmountable obstacle.

Findings made in a comparison of two industrially advanced countries — the two Germanies — showed a similar trend.[24] So did an opinion poll commissioned by a West German research institute in the mid-1970s (into life and life-style in the two Germanies). For example, to the question 'whether they felt optimistic about their future', 92 per cent in the GDR answered in the affirmative, only 74 per cent in the Federal Republic. One may then conclude that notwithstanding setbacks and mistakes, sacrifices and hardships, the nations of Eastern Europe have come a long way and their future is not bleak. Most people have a lot at stake today, the socialist society is well entrenched and supported by most of its citizens. The forces in the West who proclaim that the opinions of the dissenters or of the defectors are the same as those held by the people are either under a dangerous illusion or are out deliberately to mislead.

Notes and References

1. Wilczynski, *Economics of Socialism*, p. 95.
2. Ibid., pp. 96-7.
3. 'The Passenger Car and Socialist Economic Planning', in B. Mieczkowski (ed.), *East European Transport: Regions and Modes* (The Hague, Nijhogg 1980), pp. 257.
4. Ibid., pp. 259-60.
5. Ibid., p. 265.
6. 'How They Live in Comecon', *Current Affairs Bulletin*, vol. 57, no. 3 (1976), p. 12.
7. Ibid., p. 7.
8. Steele, *Socialism with a German Face*, 8, pp. 150-66.
9. Wilczynski, 'How They Live', p. 6.
10. Ibid., p. 12.
11. Ibid., p. 15.
12. Steele, pp. 179-80.

13. Ibid., p. 181.
14. *Osteuropa*, vol. 26, no. 3 (1977), pp. 528-48.
15. Wilczynski, *Economics of Socialism*, p. 209.
16. Ibid., pp. 210-11.
17. Ibid., pp. 212-13.
18. Hans Apel, 'Bulgarien und Griechenland, Ein Systemvergleich wirtschaftlicher und sozialer Nachkriegsentwicklung', *Osteuropa*, vol. 26 (1976), p. 273.
19. Ibid., pp. 274-6.
20. Ibid.
21. Ibid., p. 276.
22. Ibid., p. 278.
23. Ibid., p. 283.
24. Anna Hartmann *et al.* (eds.), *BRD-DDR, Vergleich der Gesellschaftssysteme*, Pahl-Rugenstein Verlag (Köln, 1971).

11 CONVERGENCE OR DIVERGENCE[1]

During the 1960s and 1970s, convergence theories enjoyed considerable popularity with a number of Western academics of varying political persuasions. They claimed that the two systems were gradually moving towards each other and that the differences that had hitherto separated the East and West were disappearing. The convergence theory certainly marked a new stage in Western scholarship on the socialist world. Until then, ever since the formation of the Soviet Union in 1917, accounts about the socialist world – virtually without exception – were not only purely negative but also usually forecasted an imminent collapse of the system. When the Bolsheviks emerged as victors from the collapse of the Tsarist empire few Western observers thought that the new rulers would survive for long. The London *Times*, for example, wrote on 10 November 1917 that the new government would be swept away by the 'first next best Kosak regiment'. The *New York Times* in the years between 1917 and 1919 predicted the collapse of the Soviet Union no less than 91 times. The German economist Werner Sombart, in an analysis of the new Soviet state, concluded in 1918 that a revolution would never be able to create a new economic system.[2] And the German sociologist Max Weber in an article on 'Domestic and Foreign Policies' declared in 1918 that Bolshevism was a 'pure military dictatorship of the corporals'.[3] He too felt that the October Revolution would not survive for longer than a few months.

History proved these early predictions wrong, but claims of an imminent collapse of the Soviet system continued. A number of middle-class economists maintained that socialism could not function in a rational manner and could never develop into a serious competitor to capitalism. As one of them wrote early in the 1930s (at the height of the great depression), capitalism was the only possible system of economic rationality, and that socialism would push production 'into a wild chaos out of which there is no other escape but a return to an economic system of more primitive cultures'.[4]

Even the astonishing victory of the Soviet Union over Nazi Germany did not immediately encourage a more realistic assessment of the economic potential created by socialism. The collapse of the old order in Eastern Europe and parts of Asia led to so-called 'containment policies' in the United States which were designed to stop the further advancement of socialism. This theory was formulated by the American diplomat George F. Kennan and, after having been passed by both the US Senate and the House of Representatives, was officially announced by President Truman on 12 March 1947. The 'Truman doctrine' was intended to protect United States interests through economic, political and, if necessary, military means. American aid for Greece and Turkey, the Marshall Plan and later the foundation of NATO were the major steps. Kennan speculated about the aims of such policy. If the Western powers were to be strong enough to contain the Soviet Union for 10 to 15 years, what would this mean for Russia? His answer was that it would lead to the collapse of Soviet society because 'no mystical, Messianic movement and particularly not that of the Kremlin can face frustration indefinitely without eventually adjusting itself in one way or another to the logic of that state of affairs'.[5] To this Kennan added a sombre picture of the conditions then prevailing in the Soviet Union: 'We have in Russia today a population which is physically and spiritually tired. The mass of the people are disillusioned, sceptical and no longer as accessible as they once were to the magical attraction which Soviet power still radiates to its followers abroad.'[6] Continuing the never-ending American fairy-tale of the imminent collapse of the Soviet economy (which enjoys a new lease of life today), Kennan also felt that the Soviet system was far too weak and fragile to impress the world with Marxist achievements. Moreover the internal structure was disintegrating and serious differences were beginning to cripple party life.

> if disunity were ever to seize and paralyse the Party, the chaos and weakness of Russian society would be revealed in forms beyond description. For Soviet power is seen as a crust concealing an amorphous mass of human beings among whom no independent organizational structure is tolerated. In Russia there is not even such a thing as local government in the western sense. The present generation of Russians have never known spontaneity of collective action. If, consequently, anything were ever to occur to disrupt the unity and efficacy of the Party as a political instrument, Soviet Russia might be changed overnight from one of the strongest to one of the weakest and most pitiable of national societies.[7]

Hence, Soviet power 'bears within it the seeds of its own decay and that sprouting of these seeds is well advanced'.[8] As Günter Rose points out, this is an astonishing misjudgement of the situation by someone who ranked among the West's top observers of Eastern Europe. The aim of the containment course to preserve the American nuclear monopoly and decisively weaken the socialist economic system was not fulfilled, however, and in the early 1950s, under John Foster Dulles, Secretary of State in the Eisenhower administration, American policies took on a more aggressive tone. Dulles described the prevailing course as 'sterile and static'. Instead of the 'negative, futile and immoral policy of containment', the US should not be frightened to sail 'close to the edge' and should be prepared at any time to stage 'a massive pre-emptive' strike at the strategic centres of the enemy. This new policy, known as the 'roll-back' policy, was academically buttressed by a series of publications by James Burnham who enjoyed a high reputation during the Eisenhower-Dulles years. Burnham insisted that the United States should not only stop the advancement of socialism but should actually aim for the complete destruction of the socialist camp.[9] Complete annihilation of communism must become the prime goal for US foreign policies. According to Burnham the Third World War had already started and soon the Cold War would submerge into total armed confrontation. He raised the possibility of an immediate attack upon the enemy to finish the business once and for all but felt that at that time a policy of internal subversion would be just as effective and less expensive. He also felt that the population was not as yet in the right frame of mind for an all-out war.[10]

The 'roll-back' policy changed with the advent of John F. Kennedy to the presidency. Not only had this extreme form of Cold War been unsuccessful throughout the 1950s but the launching of the Sputnik and the overall development in the socialist countries did not support claims that the system was getting weaker. The first publication of the 'convergence theory' occurred in the early 1960s but elements of the idea had been hinted at previously. In 1927 Werner Sombart, reanalysing and changing his original position of 1919 had this to say:

> We will have to get used to the thought that the difference between a stable regimented capitalism and a technically developed rationalized socialism is not very big and henceforth it does not really matter for the well being of man and culture whether the economy is run along socialist or capitalist lines. Important is: The nature of work is the same in both cases. One may ask oneself what is the difference between a communist or capitalist warehouse, a communist or a capitalist steel mill, or a municipal or capitalist tramway. One will not find anything substantially different. Maybe the 'consciousness' of the worker here or there is different.[11]

Convergence or Divergence

George Kennan too had to rethink his original thoughts about the chances of socialism and ten years later admitted that the economic development in the Soviet Union far surpassed anything he had thought possible. But now Kennan argued that the Soviet Union faced the stage of economic maturity which the advanced capitalist countries had reached long ago. At this stage it faced problems of organisation, workforce difficulties and slower growth areas. The end of the cult of personality and the new cultural and technical revolution created further problems. From this Kennan deduced that the Soviets would not be able to master these problems unless they pursued policies based on capitalist lines.[12]

During the 1960s two basic strands of convergence theory emerged. The more conservative one was formulated by advisers to the United States policy-makers. In essence this version of the theory argues that the two systems are coming together because the Soviet Union is moving towards a state which the United States had already reached long ago. W.W. Rostow's *Stages of Economic Growth*, which was published in 1960 and translated into 17 languages, attempted to set out a theoretical and political alternative to Marxism, to show the latter's outdatedness. Rostow's book, at the time of its publication highly acclaimed in the West, alleged that the difference between the various social systems lies primarily in the attained level of development. Hence the difference between the social systems was a difference in phases. In Rostow's opinion the United States constituted the highest stage of development in terms of production and consumption. It follows from this that all industrial nations will emulate the American model and will eventually reach America's stage of high mass consumption. According to his convergence theory, socialist society will disintegrate as soon as it reaches the state of high mass consumption because growing affluence is alleged to be incompatible with the revolutionary character of socialist ideology. Mass consumerism will lead to the embourgeoisement of socialist society. This is the essence of all convergence theories of the conservative type: Galbraith's 'technostructure', or modern industrial society, Daniel Bell's 'post-industrial society' Brzezinski's 'technotronical society' or Beraux's 'neo-technical age', all of them rest on the basic premise that the degree of accumulation and the level of income constitute the basis of society and not the issue of the ownership of the means of production.

As Eastern European critics were quick to point out, the essence of such a theory had nothing to do with convergence. It did not demonstrate that the two systems were becoming closer. Rather it predicted the eventual demise of socialism. This argument is, in other words, a diversion, merely a different prediction of the imminent end of socialism. Two of the most prominent writers on Eastern Europe in the West come to the same conclusion:

> The basic argument of the convergence theory does not mean anything else than that the Soviet Union and the United States are getting to look more alike. Changes are taking place yet this change is almost completely one sided. This thesis tacitly acquiesces in the pictures of a static America and a dynamic Soviet Union. The United States is presented as free and wealthy with the Soviet Union slowly but certainly approaching the same condition.[13]

A variation of this line is also the famous 'North-South' division replacing that of 'East-West' as the centre of future conflict, a view which enjoyed popularity in the early 1970s. In the light of recent events, no one today would put forward such a comic variation of the real conflict haunting our globe.

The second convergence theory is more liberal and also more sophisticated, but it too predicts the end of socialist society. Its eventual 'third way solution' is in essence a Western liberal, moderate social democratic interpretation of society. This theory, formulated by Jan Tilbergen, P.A. Sorokin, Walter Buckingham and others, maintains that both systems are changing. Their argument is that capitalism is becoming less and less capitalist, socialism less and less socialist and both systems are moving towards a common position. They will amalgamate in a new 'third system'. It is alleged that during this process the 'negative' aspects of both systems will disappear, the 'positive' will remain, each will absorb each other's better features until the 'optimal structure' of an ideal society is attained. According to this convergence theory, the society of the future unites elements of a socialist planned economy with those of a capitalist market economy, a workers' democracy with entrepreneurial initiative, social security and justice with a high standard of living.

The model suggested by these convergence theoreticians is in essence still a capitalist economy although some concessions are made to the achievements of the performance of socialism. Unlike Rostow's argument, which still constitutes a Cold War approach, the latter is in favour of co-existence. Wilczynski crystallises the arguments of convergence theory. He refers to the 'micro-macro tendencies'. Since the 1960s, the socialist countries have paid more attention to the previously neglected sphere of micro-economics. Capitalist countries, on the other hand, faced by the problems of social welfare, economic stagnation and inflation, have placed more emphasis on macro problems. The role of economic planning is also said to have changed. The trend away from too rigid planning in the socialist countries has been accompanied at the same time by an increase in the use of planning techniques in the Western world to promote high levels of employment, stability and social welfare. Wilczynski refers also to the role of decentralisation during the 1960s in the socialist world and the formation of ever larger economic units in the West. Further elements of this view of convergence mention the roles of management. The director in a socialist enterprise is not unlike a manager in the capitalist world. The banking system and profits are of increasing importance in the East, whereas they are of declining significance in the West. (Income disparities are said to be growing in the socialist world while they are diminishing in the West.) Other factors listed include the role of the consumer society, the mutual trade between socialist and capitalist countries and the tacit acceptance of the policy of peaceful co-existence. However Wilczynski quickly cautions the reader not to be unduly optimistic about the likelihood of convergence.

> If the foregoing instances of developments on each side have convinced the reader of the trend towards the convergence of socialism and capitalism, his enthusiasm will be tempered by the following observations. It must be pointed out that the emerging similarity of forms does not necessarily lead to substantive identity, as is illustrated, for example, by profit. Most of the modifications taking place on each side are not conscious imitations but rather selective adaptations to a variety of economic and technical changes, independent of the other system. In this process, it is easy to confuse means with the end.[14]

Not unexpectedly these theories came under strong criticism from both right and left. Right-wing academics saw in liberal convergence theories an attempt to soften the image of the 'communist totalitarian enemy', something to be avoided at all costs. A West German sociologist, for example, warned that 'a community's power to resist must be reduced if the image of the enemy power is weakened by a kind of "volonte generale"'.[15] Another West German academic argued even more strongly that 'One certainly should not have wool pulled across one's eyes by the view that Communism merely constitutes an eastern variety of "industrial society" . . . this obviously would blur the real frontiers in a most dangerous way'. Such a view would weaken the 'free world' and would promote indecisiveness, confusion and laxity towards communism. The argument that socialism would change into 'industrial society' would reduce the willingness to fight against communism which he labels as the 'most satanic of all social-religions'.[16] The notion that the battle of East and West is a battle between Christ and anti-Christ is a popular concept in the right-wing critiques of liberal convergence theories.

The Eastern European writers, in addition to claiming that the whole convergence issue is a diversionary manoeuvre, point to a series of other shortcomings. Not all the values referred to by the convergence theorists have the same meaning in socialism as in capitalism. It has already been pointed out that the profit motive means something very different in socialist society to what it does in capitalism, and the same can be said about a number of other terms. 'Goods', 'price', 'credit' and 'interest', even 'market', take on different connotations in the socialist context. As Eastern economists point out, in socialism it is not the degree of profitability of the enterprise which is the determining factor but the co-ordination of production to the best possible increase of the social product. Socialist accumulation hence means the accumulation of goods. The goal and motor of the socialist nation's economy is the optimal combination of all resources for the improvement of living conditions rather than profit. This does not allow for exploitation and alienation of labour, which socialism attempts to overcome but which capitalism because of its very nature cannot overcome. Nor can it be seriously argued that the distribution of wealth and income is narrowing in the Western world. In fact, recent years have shown that the opposite is the case. Hence most of the modifications which have occurred in the two systems are not conscious imitations but rather selective adaptations to a number of economic and technical changes which have nothing to do with the other system. As a Polish economist puts it:

> The reforms being carried out in Socialist societies have nothing in common with the convergence of Socialism and capitalism. They are merely used to perfect our system of planning and management whereby the objectives of the Socialist society can be attained in a more effective way.[17]

In essence the socialist theoreticians still argue that the Marxist law of economic development will eventually render capitalism obsolete. This is important for their concept of co-existence. It does not mean that the two systems are drawing closer together but that they exist

Convergence or Divergence

next to each other, both peacefully pursuing their own course. The fact that socialism remains as the only basis for a more humane society is not questioned. Peaceful co-existence is then looked upon as 'peaceful competition' on the economic front and Eastern socialists have little doubt of the eventual victory of socialism over capitalism.

The history of our century has shown that Karl Marx's argument that the cyclical nature of capitalist crises will lead to its demise is more accurate than many Western theoreticians would like to admit. But the course of events in the years 1914 to 1945 has also shown that the old system will not end with a whimper. The first wave of success for socialism in the first half of this century was accompanied by the violent death of over 100 million people. As Western difficulties increase, with some countries having already reached the stage of the great depression of the 1930s, those forces in the United States who advocate a preemptive nuclear strike while America has still the upper hand may win out. Some comments by the American administration in recent years hint at such a possibility.

If successful it would indeed end the threat of socialism for a long time. If unsuccessful, the law of economics may win out. Whether there will be anyone left to enjoy the new Jerusalem is a different question.

Notes and References

1. For a detailed account of the points summarised in this chapter note Günter Rose, *Konvergenz der Systeme* (Pahl-Rugenstein Verlag, Köln, 1970); *'Industriegesellschaft'* und *Konvergenztheorie* (Deutscher Verlag der Wissenschaften, Berlin, GDR, 1974); Wilfried von Bredow, *Vom Antagonismus zur Konvergenz* (Metzner, Frankfurt, Main, 1972).
2. Werner Sombart, *Sozialismus und soziale Bewegung* (Fischer, Jena, 1919), p. 146; quoted in Rose, 'Industriegesellschaft', p. 76.
3. Max Weber, *Gesammelte Politische Schriften*, p. 280 quoted in Rose, *Industriegesellschaft*, p. 77.
4. Ibid., p. 78.
5. George F. Kennan, 'The Sources of Soviet Conduct', *Foreign Affairs*, vol. 4 (1947), p. 582.
6. Ibid., p. 577.
7. Ibid., pp. 579-80.
8. Ibid., p. 580.
9. James Burnham, *The Coming Defeat of Communism* (Jonathan Cape, London, 1950).
10. Ibid.
11. Werner Sombart, *Das Wirtschaftsleben im Zeitalter der Kapitalismus*, vol. III, (Duncker und Humblot, Munich, Leipzig, 1927), pp. 1014 ff., quoted in Rose, *Industriegesellschaft*, p. 78.
12. The Reith Lectures, BBC broadcast, 'Russia, the Atom and the West',

published in German as *Russland, der Westen und die Atomwaffe* (Ullstein, Frankfurt/Main, 1958), p. 10.

13. Zbigniew Brzezinski and Samuel P. Huntington, 'Die Sowiet Union und die Vereinigten Staaten: Konvergenz oder Evolution der politischen und sozialen Strukture?', *Europa-Archiv*, vol. 12 (1964), p. 428.

14. Wilczynski, *Economics of Socialism*, p. 217.

15. Johannes Christian Papalekas, 'Die westliche Gesellschaft und die kommunistische Drohung', *Bergedorfer Protokolle*, vol. 5 (Hamburg, West Berlin), p. 44 quoted in Rose, p. 313.

16. Wilhelm Röpke, *Gegen die Brandung* (Albert Hunold, Zürich, Stuttgart, 1959), p. 320.

17. Quoted in Wilczynski, *Economics of Socialism*, p. 217.

12 RECREATION AND ENTERTAINMENT

Recently the Hungarian sociologist Zsuzsa Ferge analysed the current state of society in Hungary[1] (and socialist society in general) and in the concluding chapter of her study she pondered over the direction society would take in future. How can socialist society set about achieving individual happiness within society as a whole? She stated that the most pressing needs in Hungary have by and large now been overcome. Hunger, mass squalor, precarious living conditions, general scarcity have become problems of the past. Some hardships still remain, especially as far as housing is concerned, but these will be overcome; the majority of people are becoming well off, even prosperous.

This leads to the question of how the new prosperity will be utilised. What should be the aims in future? In answering this Ferge points out that so far we know only 'one model of prosperity' — that of advanced capitalist countries. In her argument this does not really correspond to a socialist ideal because, as critics of the affluent society stress, affluence still has its drawbacks — both for those privileged to enjoy it and still more for those in advanced Western countries who are deprived of it. Hence the basic values of capitalist society such as acquisitiveness, consumerism, individualism in its extreme Western form (individual advancement at the cost of hardship to others) and an exaggerated work ethos 'can hardly be seen as eminently socialist ones'.[2] Although elements of all this will carry over into socialist society, these values are essentially negative, non-socialist: what is needed is a positive socialist way of life. Ferge then suggests some essential steps which would have to be taken. First, there is need to reorganise the division of work and so to overcome the socially divisive features of work. By mobilising more human abilities, more and more varied needs are aroused. And if work is less confining and more life-enhancing for a number of people, all other aspects of life can change more easily towards better standards. On this basis, present inequalities can be overcome, leading to higher living standards for a large strata which would help to eliminate the present tendencies of invidious differentiation. This would also achieve a more plentiful and egalitarian redistribution whilst at the same time the utilisation of collective funds would affect consumption patterns and the way of life more directly. If all this is successfully applied, the following results would be achieved:

They promote collective mobility by creating less differentiated frameworks for everyday life and by developing more and more varied needs and abilities in everybody;

They strengthen or create a basis for social relations that may be a form of solidarity because they weaken the motives for acquisitiveness, competitiveness, invidious attitudes;

They contribute to the humanization of needs. In fact, on the basis of these two conditions the autotelic, self-contained nature of consumption and of ways of consuming may be restored. In class societies, the coverage of the diverse needs took place in a way which transcended the original aim: the way of covering the need almost always became impregnated with social overtones expressing or accentuating the social difference. Thus the coverage of needs ceased to be an end in itself, but was transmuted into a means of expressing social standing. By the same token, the objects (whether material or not) of need-satisfaction ceased to be simple means to that end. By acquiring symbolic overtones, they themselves became ends, possessing an intrinsic value. The humanization of needs implies the reversal of these trends, which becomes possible, if and only if, the present social determinants, based on basic social inequalities, weaken and the needs, the ways and means of the coverage of human needs, become freer, more autonomous expressions of human personality.[3]

These are obviously long-term goals — the idea of a communist utopia based on cultural rather than materialistic values is still a long way in the future. For some time to come people in the socialist countries will still follow more mundane pursuits in their spare time rather than concentrating primarily upon the intellectual enrichment of their lives. The visitor to the socialist countries will soon detect that the myth of the allegedly 'dull life behind the Iron Curtain' sometimes propagated in the West does not hold true.

Notwithstanding the post-Second World War changes, all the countries have maintained and fostered their traditional ethnic culture. The Hungarian life-style, for example, which long enjoyed a reputation for gaiety and easy living, has not changed — only more people are able to enjoy it now. The visitor will note that at first sight Budapest, the second centre of the old Danube monarchy, differs little from Vienna. Buildings of the Austro-Hungarian past still crowd both sides of the Danube, interrupted by modern hotels, office buildings and supermarkets. There are merely fewer cars and the shops are not quite as lavishly stocked. Situated in the middle of the Danube is Margrete Island, a large recreation reserve with swimming pools and other sports facilities, parks, children's playgrounds, open theatres and hotels. On a summer weekend the whole of Budapest seems to retire to this place. The Hungarians certainly seem to enjoy life. A wide choice of restaurants offers high-quality meals at far below Western prices. At night the Danube echoes to the sound of music, 'disco steamers' can be heard and on other ships Hungarian bands play Western tunes from jazz to pop. Talking to a group of students and teachers in a Budapest beer hall, one has the impression that Hungary has come a long way since 1956. They felt happy with their country and their society. A lot has been achieved in transforming a backward agrarian country with a large proportion of its inhabitants in a poverty stricken state, to a modern industrialised economy offering educational opportunities for everyone, job security and a comparatively high standard of living. How do the people feel towards the government? Kadar has the respect and even affection of most people; he governs effectively without the personality cult of a Tito or a Ceaucescu.

The capital of Hungary's northern neighbour, Prague, the third metropolis of the old Austro-Hungarian empire, has also remained a beautiful city. Thousands of tourists stroll through the streets of old Prague and every hour a multitude of cameras are focused ready for the appearance of the Apostles at the old Town Hall. Compared to Budapest, the range of goods at the major department stores is slightly disappointing but food shops offer appetising goods at cheap prices. At night Prague offers a wide range of entertainment; the pubs of the old town are one of the major tourist attractions. Compared to Hungary the overall atmosphere is quieter. Resentment about 1968 still pervades the atmosphere. As someone commented, the Czechs have reverted to the old soldier Schweyk mentality, taking things quietly and enjoying life for what it has to offer. There is a lot on offer. Outside Prague the mountainous countryside, with its old villages and towns, is once again attracting tourists from all parts of Europe.

Budapest and Prague were lucky to experience comparatively moderate destruction during the Second World War. Poland, on the other hand, experienced the massive devastation caused by the German retreat before the Red Army. The Polish achievement in reconstructing their destroyed cities is unique in Europe. In Warsaw, large parts of the old town have been rebuilt using old drawings and photographs as the architectural basis for the reconstruction. The old parts of Gdansk were so well rebuilt that Volker Schlondorff's film of Günther Grass's famous novel *The Tin Drum* (which won the Cannes prize) could be filmed in virtually the original settings of the novel.

Sports and gymnastic activities are widely provided in all socialist countries both indoor and outdoor. In Berlin, for example, every suburb has its own indoor swimming pool with sauna and gymnastic rooms. All citizens, not only the top athletes, benefit from these sports facilities – indeed, the rather spectacular sport performances of some of the socialist countries can only be explained by this generous provision of sporting facilities. As has been stated already, union-funded accommodation is available at all mountain and sea tourist centres and every week citizens, in parties or alone, participate in climbing, mountain walks or a simple stroll through what is still in part a comparatively unspoiled countryside.

As everywhere in Europe, in summertime the bulk of the people head for a seaside resort and the result is, of course, overcrowding everywhere. Every spot on the coast around the Baltic, Adriatic or Black Seas, indeed every bay and lake, is besieged with tents and holiday homes. In the GDR, as in West Germany, nude bathing has become predominant, but this is a rare scene among the more modest Poles. In Bulgaria, the government has decided that the hot-blooded character of its male population makes it essential to separate the sexes for nude bathing. The leading European spectator sports enjoy as much popularity here as they do in the West. Big soccer games draw large crowds and the Czechs are as keen on ice hockey as the Canadians.

Crime is a problem although it is not of Western proportions. 'Crimes against the state', such as embezzlement and misappropriation of funds, are on the increase in all socialist societies. A GDR weekly column stated:

> with so many country cottages it is obvious that the gates and fences have been illegally acquired. Anyone can see that, but no one says a word, probably because so many people have also helped themselves from society's 'great pot'. The courts uncover occasional cases of massive corruption, usually by factory managers who inflate their payrolls and pocket non-existent workers' wages, or account for payments for materials that were ordered but never supplied.[4]

A Western tourist is less likely to be the victim of crime in Eastern Europe but he would be well advised not to enter into illegal currency exchange deals. He will often be approached to exchange western currency at rates far more favourable than the official exchange rate. Not only is this highly illegal and punished with substantial fines; he may

Recreation and Entertainment 167

also fall victim to a confidence trick and find that he has been taken for an expensive ride.

New ways of dealing with crime are being tested in the East. Steele presents an example of a local 'disputes commission':

> People were brought together for a discussion, survivors, local people and the police participated. The accident had produced one young man's death and injuries to eight others when the Wartburg car they had crammed into crashed. All of them had been drinking. Although the driver who died was the main guilty party, several people thought the eight passengers should lose their licences. Others thought the people in the pub where the young men were drinking should have spotted the potential danger and warned them against driving. The major concluded that everyone in the community should feel some responsibility. A pious platitude? A green light to the busybodies in any community to become more active? Or a genuine attempt to awaken more of a collective spirit? Probably it was a mixture of all three.[5]

Nightlife is inexpensive and perhaps best described as 'clean fun'. There are bands, dancing, people meet; but whereas in Western Europe pornography has reached a new peak – or low – with the ill-famed peep-holes, striptease and hard-core pornographic films, these are outlawed in all socialist countries. And so is prostitution. They all constitute an affront to the dignity and position of women but – with the possible exception of the GDR – the Western tourist will soon notice that, at least as far as prostitution is concerned, there is a considerable discrepancy between the noble goal of the law and the sombre reality of the practice. Here, again because of the currency situation, hotels for Western tourists are particularly popular targets for local prostitutes.

Berlin has become the symbol for the differences between the socialist and the capitalist world. During the first decades after the division of Germany, West Berlin won the test of comparison very easily. West Berliners recovered much more quickly than did East Berliners. Whereas West Berlin could soon boast affluence and even splendour, East Berlin seemed to fall steadily behind. Today the difference is not so glaring. Unemployment, deterioration of the housing situation – which affects young people in particular and the hundreds of thousands of *Gastarbeiter* – and affiliated problems have removed the glamour. At the same time 'the other side' of the city has picked up. The area around the Alexanderplatz, the television tower (the second largest in the world) and the Hotel Berlin shows that the GDR has much to boast about. In fact some visitors to Berlin today feel that there is too much ostentation all around. The difference in night life is enormous. Strolling along Kurfürstendamm in West Berlin one entertainment joint follows the other. Sophisticated nightclubs and restaurants provide a vast range of food, dance halls, cabaret and variety entertainment, pub after pub, not to mention peep-hole parlours, striptease joints and large-scale prostitution. Compared to this the night life of East Berlin is modest. There are a number of nightclubs with sophisticated cabaret, pubs, friendly beer cellars of the old Berlin kind and dance halls, but they are considerably fewer than in West Berlin. The gap is narrowing but with the country becoming more affluent, supply in East Berlin is as yet not up to demand. The red light district is totally missing and so is the sight of 13- and 14-year-old girls prostituting themselves as they do around the West Berlin Zoo station to obtain cash for heroin. Although some addictive drugs are available in the East, there is no drug problem – unlike West Berlin, where more than 100 people per year die from heroin addiction.

Surprisingly, there are two race courses in East Berlin. The old Hoppegarten in the South-east part of Berlin has been in operation since 1922, and is used for racing on Saturdays. The Karlshorst Rennbahn is used for trotting races on Sunday. All newspapers publish form guides – assessments of track conditions – in their sports sections. Horses, however, belong to nationalised stables. The racing crowds are quite large although there are no bookmakers – only totalisator gambling. Bets are restricted to 10 marks. Surprisingly too in the GDR (and in other socialist countries), there are also games such as Lotto. All of this does not really indicate that the progress in Eastern Europe towards a non-materialistic New Jerusalem is all that rapid.

A visitor to most of the socialist countries discussed in this book, if he is willing to adopt an objective stance, will have to concede that much has been achieved. No doubt there have been many mistakes and setbacks and many problems still remain. Not long ago a Polish academic, Ian Szczepanski, attended a Western conference and gave a paper which is well worth quoting in detail.[6] The conference guest appreciated being given the opportunity to speak 'to so many distinguished scholars' who by virtue of their 'intellect, vigour and determination' had secured for themselves a prominent place in their own countries. He felt, as he was not a member of the Western scholarly community, that the conference might like to hear about an Eastern European view of their field of studies. He stressed that he was talking for no one but himself, as a sociologist, trying to discover the 'universal rules of societal life and human behaviour'. Szczepanski felt greatly encouraged that a search for a spirit of collaboration was going on among scholarly communities on both sides of the ideological dividing line, but he did not think that it was easy to achieve co-operation in all fields. As he pointed out, it is no secret that in the past a good deal of research stemmed not from a spirit of co-operation but of confrontation. For example, it was by no means accidental that the rapid growth of Soviet and Eastern European studies took place during the Cold War. In fact a special issue of *Survey* dealing with the current state of affairs of Eastern studies raised the question whether further development was to be impeded by the ceasing of East-West conflict. The Polish sociologist also doubted whether true scholarly objectivity was the guiding principle of many Eastern researchers.

> Legitimate ideological differences, moreover, are often transformed into deep-seated personal prejudices. Efforts to bridge this gap have often run into a barrier of widely held stereotypes. This is also very much true of western scholarship. Let me give you a personal example. When, in 1970, I published in the United States my book *Polish Society* (in which I tried to explain to western readers as impartially as I could the changes in my country) it was abruptly dismissed by a reviewer in the *Canadian Slavonic Papers* as an effort by a prominent member of the Communist establishment to pose as a dispassionate social scientist.[7]

The argument continued, quoting Western sociologists, that perhaps conflict and war are more conducive to advancing a knowledge of opponents than friendship and co-operation. However, as he correctly stressed, they also produce so many negative effects that it is hardly the best way to advance knowledge. Although ideological differences between the two systems will – and should – exist, they should not bar attempts to find solutions together to the many shared problems of the global village.

> Your Conference meets at a time when the gravity of various world crises has been vividly impressed upon us. We are faced today with the ecological perils, the demographic explosion, the energy shortage, galloping inflation, declining food supplies, the instability of the international monetary system, and political difficulties in many countries resulting in military takeovers. In such circumstances broad comparative studies, conducted without any prejudice and aimed at

the discovery of the basic forces operating in the different societies, regardless of their systems, are more important than ever ... I have not been able, of course, to evaluate systematically the hundreds of books and thousands of articles published in the West on Eastern Europe. However, I have looked at a good many of your more important studies in the social sciences, especially those published in recent years after the end of the cold war. In doing so I have repeatedly asked myself, what do they contribute to an understanding of the Soviet and the various East European societies? What are their political overtones and what assumptions are tacitly accepted as obvious? What is the image of the socialist countries and are these countries portrayed as enemies or partners? How many of the books are aimed at opposing Communism in Eastern Europe, and how many strive to provide for accommodation and detente? Finally, what practical recommendations do they contain for expanded East-West cooperation? I do not intend to answer these questions in a comprehensive fashion. I would rather like to encourage my North American and West European colleagues, who know the existing literature better than I do, to try to pose these queries to themselves ... I have to admit however, that my overall impressions of Western literature on Eastern Europe are not too encouraging ... It would seem to me that the Marxist thesis of conditioning the social sciences by social interests has been more than amply demonstrated by the Western research on Eastern Europe. In most works the assumption is accepted, either implicitly or explicitly, that Communism, and indeed anything which is different for the Western political system, is in some way 'abnormal' ... [8]

Szczepanski continued with the claim that the actual transformation of establishing socialism and the various social forces involved in this process are virtually unknown in the West. Nor is there any discussion of patterns of behaviour, values, traditions: 'in short the entire microstructure of society is almost completely absent in western literature'. The omission of these extremely important aspects of life in these societies, he reasoned, not without justification, greatly impoverished the picture presented by standard Western literature. Finally, he strongly backed the need for co-operation.

A new climate of international scholarly cooperation is possible, and in fact, is badly needed. I am convinced that in this respect many East European scholars share my views. I would like to reiterate, however, that such cooperation will be possible only if our political and ideological differences are mutually accepted and respected. There is no longer a place for ideological crusades. Instead we should focus our attention on improving our methodological tools and our scientific results. This is the way to contribute to the better knowledge of the contemporary world and its urgent problems.[9]

People in Eastern Europe are aware of what has been achieved. The recent setbacks in Poland cannot blur this fact. They have more to lose than is often claimed in the West. There is in the West an obsessive preoccupation with people who dissent and with the difficulties facing Eastern Europe, to the almost complete exclusion of the views of the rest of the population on the achievements that have occurred. Television programmes on the Anglo-Saxon commercial networks are more often geared to producing advertising revenues than to providing the public with an informative picture.

There are people in Eastern Europe who no doubt still bitterly resent the course of recent history and who will do so for some time. But even they prefer the present system if political changes meant another armed conflict. With the spectre of a nuclear holocaust looming, they share the fears of many people in Europe today. It is not possible for the outside observer to evaluate what is really going on in the defence-planning and decision-making departments of the superpowers, but most West European statesmen take the recent disarmament offers by the Soviet Union as genuine. And to the ever-growing peace movement in Western Europe the escalation of the conflict has not been caused by the Soviet Union.

So the Cold War is still going on, if not getting worse. The former foreign affairs adviser to President Carter, and member of the human rights association, Brzezinski declared in an interview with the Paris-based *International Herald Tribune* that he would have no hesitation in pressing the nuclear button.[10] The current American administration regards a nuclear war as possible — and sections of the Western press add their share to the escalation of the conflict. From the latter one may expect no better. Many of the Western Europeans think tanks on Eastern Europe, especially those in the USA, are more interested in continuing the conventional 'Kremlinologist' approach rather than the task of fostering understanding of the other system. This is even more regrettable. Recently a textbook produced for the United States tertiary market was widely circulated and advertised. It is called *Modern Europe*[11] and claims to deal with twentieth-century European history.

In reality, however, it is a return to the Cold War anti-Soviet account which matches anything published in the early 1950s, culminating in the totally absurd allegation that Czechoslovakia in 1968 faced a return to a peasant-based economy. This does make the gloomiest prognostications seem to come true. The book argues for an end to detente policies as they foster Soviet aggression. What are such historical falsifications to achieve? Is it 1914 or 1939 again? Are we being mentally prepared for such a result?

It is hoped that such mistakes are only an academic oversight.

Notes and References

1. Zsuzsa Ferge, *A Society In The Making* (Penguin, Harmondsworth, 1979), Ch. 9, pp. 306-26.
2. Ibid., p. 318.
3. Ibid., pp. 325-6.
4. Steele, *Socialism with a German Face*, p. 156.
5. Ibid., p. 157.
6. *Canadian Slavonic Review*, vol. 16 (1974), pp. 530-8.
7. Ibid., p. 532.
8. Ibid., pp. 532-4.
9. Ibid., p. 537.
10. *International Herald Tribune*, 10 October 1977.
11. Richard Pipes, *Modern Europe* (Dorsey Press, Illinois, 1981).

INDEX

action programme 99, 104
Aczel, Gyorgy 64
Adenauer, Konrad 29
Afghanistan 7
Albania 10; inter-war years 11, 13, 18; People's Republic 20-2, 48, 83, 88, establishment 20-2
'Anti-Fascist Council for the Liberation of Yugoslavia' (AVNOJ) 19
Antonescu, Ion 26
Arrow Cross 51
Athens 151
Auschwitz 16-17
Australia 81, 108, 123, 141, 143
Austria 11, 100, 114
Austro-Hungarian empire 126, 164, 165; disintegration 10; economic performance 14; losses in First World War 12; *see also* Danube monarchy, Hapsburg

Bahro, Rudolf 99, 100
Balli Kombetar 20
Baltic 37, 118, 166
Belgrade 12
Belsen 16
Benes, Eduard 28
Berlin: blockade 29, 38-9; June 1953 45, 48; nightlife and recreation 166-8; Wall 69-70, 72, 80
Berlin-Marzahn 144
Bessarabia 10, 11
Betriebsparteiorganisation (BPO) 74
Black Sea 166
Bolshevik Revolution 11; *see also* Russia, October Revolution
Bolsheviks 154
Brandt, Willy 80, 88, 110; government 7, 47
Bratislava 106
Brest 18
Brezhnev, Leonid 126; doctrine 111
Britain 123; position of women 145; post Second World War Labour Government 37, 38; *see also* Great Britain, United Kingdom
Broz, Josip 19; *see also* Tito
Brzezinski, Zbigniew 110, 157, 171

Bucharest 26, 65, 89
Budapest 11, 65, 164-5; October 1956 51
Bulgaria 10, 15; inter-war years 12, 14, 15, 18
Bulgarian People's Republic; domestic issues 148-52, living standards 140-1, 149, 151, per capita income 138, 143, social services 144, 150; economics 22, 83, 89-90, 118-19, 122, agriculture 90, 122, planned economy 35, 39, 48; establishment (of socialist government) 18, 21, 22; part in 1968 CSSR occupation 99, 110, 111
Burnham, James 156
Byrnes, James F. 37

Canada 7, 140-1, 166
car production 139-40
Carter, Jimmy 126, 171
Ceaucescu, Nicolae 86, 88-91, 120
cetnik 19
'Charta 77' 63
China 89, 91
Churchill, Sir Winston 22, 37
Cierna 106
co-existence 160, 161
Coja, Ian 91
Cold War 7, 40, 62, 169, 172; between two Germanies 28, 69, 80; Berlin issue 29, 38-9, 68; historiography 36-7, 156, 158
Cominform 40
Comintern 35
Congress of Writers (CSSR) 96, 97, 98
consumerism 139, 157
'consumer revolution 142
'containment policies' 38, 156
convergence theory 101, 156, 158-9
Council of Mutual Economic Advancement (CMEA) 55, 70, 73, 89-91, 95, 124; disagreement with Romania 83-6, 88; living standards 66, 141, 143, 144
crime in Eastern Europe 166-7

173

Croatia 11, 126, 134; 'independent State of Croatia' 16
Croatian Peasant Party 12
Curzon Line 12
Czech and Slovak Socialist Republic (CSSR): Communist Party 93, 99, 105, 106, 109, 111; Central Committee 97-8, crisis of 1968 8, 87, 92, 115, 165, 172, course of events 98-100, occupation by Warsaw Pact troops 99, 110-11, opinion polls 107-11, reform model 75, 102-3, 105, 110; economic development 73, 90, 93-4, 95-7, 140, agricultural production 94-5, 97, 122, disagreement with Romania 83, 84, 85, loans from West 119; living standards 66, 118, 140-2, 144, per capita income 66, 138, 143
Czechoslovakia: inter-war years 10, 11, 17-18, dismemberment and German occupation 12, 13, 15, 16, 28, economic development 14, 15; post World War Two period 19, 28, 35, 44-5, economic development 34-5, 39, 43
Czechoslovak People's Party (CSL) 109
Czechoslovak Socialist Party 109

Danube 164, 165
Danube monarchy 10, 164; *see also* Austro-Hungarian empire, Hapsburg
Dej, Gheorgiou 84, 86
Democratic Front (Poland) 24
Democratic League of Women (DFD) 74
de-Stalinisation 116
Die Distel 80
Dimitrov, Georgi 21
Dubcek, Alexander 98, 104, 105, 112; government 100, 106
Dulles, John Foster 156

East Berlin 166-9; *see also* Berlin
'economic levers' 71
Eisenhower administration 156
Engels, Friedrich 56
Eulenspiegel 80
extermination of Jewish people 15, 16

Fascism 10; *see also* Italy, Nazism

fascists 10, 16, 65, 126
'final solution' 16-17
Finland 100
First World War 9-11, 14, 17, 115, 126
Fourth Writers Congress 102
France 124, 143; Marshall Plan 38
Free German Youth League (FDJ) 74
Frejka, Ludvik 41
Fulton (Missouri) 37

Gabai, Alexander 11
Gabor, Pal 65
Galbraith, John Kenneth 157
Gdansk 115, 118, 165
German Democratic Republic: domestic issues, child-care and education 77, 78, confrontation 46-8, consumerism 79-80, 141-4, formation and early years 28-30, housing 79, 144-5, living standards 66, 77, 79-80, 152, rest and recreation 79, 167-8, social policies 79, 144-5, thaw 97; economics 43, 70-3, 82, 122, 140, agriculture 73, 121, 124, aid from Soviet Union 48, difficulties 45-6, 68-9, disagreement with Romania 83, 84, 85, loans from West 119, management 70-3, New Economic Model 71-2, theory 75-7; foreign affairs 41, 80-1, and Czechoslovakia 99, 106, 110, 111, and Romania 87, 88, *see also* Soviet zone
German empire 10-12
Germany: anti-Soviet tradition 30; defeat and division 10, 24, 28-9, 37, 68; Federal Republic of (West Germany) 29, 88, 111, 141, anti-communism 159-60, comparisons with GDR 73, 74, 78, 145, 152, conflict with GDR 46, 47, 68-9, economics 45, 46, 123, 143, 144, foreign policy 106, 110-11, *see also* Hallstein doctrine, Yugoslav guest workers 136-7; Nazi-period 13, 15-16, *Grossraum* economy 15, *Lebensraum* philosophy 16
Gerö, Erno 50, 51, 54, 55
Gestapo 16
Gierek, Eduard 117, 118
Gomulka, Wladislaw 41, 50, 116, 117 118

Index

Gossnab 59
Gottwald, Klement 28, 45, 93
Great Britain 15; *see also* Britain, United Kingdom
Greece 66, 135-6, 141, 155; per capita income 143-4; study of living standards 148-52
Groza, Petr 26, 27

Hallstein doctrine 80, 88, 110
Hapsburg dynasty 9
Hapsburg empire 10
Harriman, W. Averall 37
Helsinki accords 7, 62, 89
Heydrich, Reinhard 16
Hitler government 12
Hohenzollern 9
Honecker, Erich 79, 145
Honecker, Margret 145
Horthy, Miklos 11-12
Hoxha, Enver 20
Hungarian Democratic Women's Movement 55
Hungarian People's Republic; culture 102, 106, domestic issues 7, 60-1, 92, liberal reforms 62-4, 97, living standards 66, 140-4, social life 163-5; economics 89-90, 118, 119, 138, agriculture 49-50, 56, 59-60, 73, 122, 124, New Economic mechanism 57-8, 102, 132, 133, planned economy 35, 39, 48, Romanian issue 83, 91; establishment of socialist government 19; part in occupation of CSSR 99, 110; uprising of 1956 48-52, 54-5, 99, 115
Hungarian Socialist Workers' Party (SzMP) 54, 55
Hungarian Workers' Party (MAP) 50, 54, 55
Hungary: inter-war years 10-11, 14, 15, 18; Second World War 15, 16, 27, 31
Husak, Gustav 112

India 135
Indonesia 141
International Herald Tribune 171
'Iron Curtain' 37, 45, 164
Israel-Arab conflict 89
Italy 66, 143-4; fascist policies 13, 16, 20

Jancso, Miklos 64-5
Japan 123, 141, 143
Jodl, Miroslav 106
Johnson, Hewlett 32

Kadar, Janos 66, 92, 93, 103, 112; government 7, 56, 63, Hungarian uprising 50-1, 54, 55, popularity 64, 165
Kafka, Franz 102
Kafka conference 97, 98
Kapital 57
Kardelj, Eduard 130
Karolyi, Mihaly 11, 12
Katowice 118
Kennan, George F. 28, 37, 155, 157
Kennedy, John F. 69, 156
Kolkhoz-type farms 44
Kombinate 70, 71
Kosovo 134
Kovacs, Andras 65
'Kremlin-Round' 110
Kulak-type farms 44
Kun, Bela 11, 12, 18
Kunfi, Sigismund 11

Latvia 17
Legalitat 20
Leipzig 48, 65
Lengyel, Jozsef 64
Lenin, V.I. 56
Lidice 16
Lithuania 12, 17
Ljubitlana 129
'Llublin government' 23
London, Artur 41
'London Poles' 22, 23, 24
Lukacz, Georg 11
Lusatian Serbs 79
Luxemburg, Rosa 111

Macedonia 18, 134
Magdeburg 48
Majdanek 16
Margrete Island 164-5
Marshall Plan 29, 38, 40, 155
Marx, Karl 57, 132, 161
Marxism-Leninism 53, 66, 104
Marxist theories 147, 157, 160, 170; on agriculture 56; intensive to extensive growth 57
Meyerling 65
Mihailovic, Anton 19
Mikolajczyk, Stanislaw 24, 25

Minsk 12
Mlynar, Zdenek 103, 104
Molotov, Vyacheslav Mikhaylovich 38
Montenegro 18, 134
Moravia 44
Moravia-Ostrava 45
Moscow 28, 85, 91
Moscow Olympics 7
Munich 1938 93

Nagy, Ference 27
Nagy, Imre 49-50, 54-5
Nagy, Janos 62
'National Democratic Block' (Romania) 26
'National Front' 103-4
'National Liberation Movement' (Albania) 20
National Peasant Party (Hungary) 27
National Socialism (Nazism) 16, 23, 29; defeat 33, 45, 154
'Nation's National Council' (KRN) 23
Nemeth, Laszlo 64
New Economic Mechanism 58-60
New Left 36
New York Times 154
nightlife in Eastern Europe 167-8
Nixon, Richard M. 89
North Atlantic Treaty Organisation (NATO) 7, 155
'North-South conflict' 158
Novotny, Antonin 93, 96-8, 103-4, 107
Nowogrodek 18

Oder-Neisse line 24, 88
Opava 45
Ostpolitik 7
Ottoman empire 148; *see also* Turkish empire

Paris 38
Paris Commune 9
partisan resistance movement 16, 19, 126
'Patriotic Front' 21, 22
Pauker, Anna 41
Pavelic, Ante 16
Pazsgay, Hungarian minister for culture 63
Peasant Party (Hungary) 27
Peasant Party (SL), Poland 23
People's Assembly (Bulgaria) 21
People's Chamber (GDR) 70

'People's committees' (Yugoslavia) 19
'People's Democratic Front' (Romania) 27
'People's Front' (Yugoslavia) 20
'People's Liberation Army' (Bulgaria) 21
Petöfi circle 50
Pilsudski, Josef 12, 13
Planned Economy 31-3, 39
Plzen 44
Poland: early history 114, 115; inter-war years 10-12, 14-15, 18, 115; World War Two 16, 165
Polish People's Republic: domestic issues, Catholic Church 116, 117, 120, 124, literary revival 52, 97, 102, 106, 117, living standards 138, 140-4, Poznan riots 48, 116, recent events 7, 112, 123, 147, 171; economics 8, 83, 89-90, agricultural problems 120-4, 135, planned economy 31, 33-4, 39; establishment 13, 19, 23-7, 46
Polish Social Democrats (PPS) 23
Polish United Workers' Party 116, 118
Polish Worker Party (PPR)
Portugal 66, 143
Prague 40, 110, 111, 165
'Prague Spring' 96, 98, 99
Pravda 104
prostitution 167
Protectorates of Bohemia and Moravia 16
Prussia 11, 114

Radic, Stjepan 12, 13
'Radical School' 36
railway density 14
Rajk, Laszlo 41
Rakosi, Matyas 11, 48-50, 54-5, 65
Reagan administration 124
Red Army 12, 18, 21, 23, 28; defeating Germans 15, 17, 165
Research Council for Questions of Germany's Reunification 46
Revai, Joszef 54
Romania: inter-war years 10-11, 13-16, 18-19
Romanian People's (since 1965, Socialist) Republic: domestic issues 26-7, 41, 92, 140-4; economics 89-91, 118-19, agriculture 31, 122, planned economy

Index

35-6, 39, 48, 83-4; foreign policies 8, 88-9; 'national communism' 87
Romanian Workers' Party 27, 85
Romanov dynasty 9
Roosevelt, Theodore 22, 37
Rostow, Walt Whitman 157, 158
Rude Pravo 41
Russian empire 10-12, 114; revolution of 1905 9; October Revolution 11, 17, 99, 154
Ruthenia 11, 18

Sanatescu, Constantin 26
Second World War 10, 14, 26, 28, 126; agriculture before 60, 122; death toll and destruction 15, 17, 31, 115, 165; post-war changes 18, 164
Sejm 13
Sejna affair 109
Serbia 10-11, 19, 134
Sik, Ota 101-2, 104
Silesia 34, 115, 118
Simone-Katz, Andre 41
Sino-Soviet conflict 88
Slansky trials 40-1, 99
Slavonic Untermenschen 16
Slovakia 11, 15-16
'Slovakian Republic' 16
Slovenia 31, 126, 134
Sobobor 16
Socialist Unity Party (SED) 29, 46, 74, 79
Sofia 151
Solidarity 123
Solzhenitsyn, Alexander 64
Sombart, Werner 154, 156
Soviet-Czechoslovakian friendship treaty 93
Soviet Union (USSR): economics 118-19, 122, 138, 155, 157, living standards 140-4; inter-war years 11, 154; relations to People's Republics, Czechoslovakia 1968 93, 99, 106, 108, 110, economic issues 48, 70, 84, 85, 89, Hungary 1956 50, 52, role in establishing 7, 21-2, 28, 35-6, 45, 46; relations to West 28, 29, 36-8, 171; relations to Yugoslavia 40, 52, 126; World War Two 16, 33, 154
Soviet-zone (of Germany) 19, 28, 29, 32, 45; *see also* German Democratic Republic
Sputnik 156
Stalin, Josef 40, 41, 111, 147; death 41, 49
Stalinism 65
Stalinists 98, 116, 80; trials 93, 97
Stamvalishy, Alexander 12
Stettin 37
Sturm-Staffel (SS) 16-17
Stutthof 16
Sudeten-Germans 12
Sudeten Nazi Party 12
Svitak, Juan 105
Svoboda, Ludvik 104
Sweden 15, 123, 143
Switzerland 143
Szczecin 120

the thaw 52, 97
The Tin Drum 165
The Two Thousand Words 106
'third-way' theory 75, 101, 158
'Third World War' 156
Times (London) 154
Tito 19, 40-1, 126-7, 130, 137
Transylvania 11
Treblinka 16, 17
Truman, Harry S. 28, 155; administration 36-7, 38
Tsarist empire 154; *see also* Russian empire
Turkey 135, 155
Turkish empire 10; *see also* Ottoman empire

Ukraine 12, 17
Ulbricht, Walter 46, 69, 93
United Kingdom 21, 31, 66, 143; *see also* Britain, Great Britain
United Nations 37
United Nations Relief and Rehabilitation Administration (UNRRA) 31
United States of America (USA) 7, 141, 143, 144, 145; conflict with Socialist World 116, 124, 154-5, 171; cold war 36-8; nuclear threat 40, 161; post World War Two policies 21, 29, 39, 135
Ustasa 16

Varga, Bela 27
Vas, Zolan 49
Vereinigung Volkseigener Betriebe (VVB's) 70, 71, 72, 76

Versailles peace treaty 12, 115
Vetseras, Maria 65
Vienna 65, 126, 164
Vojvodina 134
Volksdeutsche 46
Volkseigener Betrieb (VEB) 70, 73

Warsaw 12, 31, 65, 165, 116; letter 106; uprising 23-4; Pact 50-1, 110, 112
Weber, Max 154
Wehrmacht 16
Weimar Republic 12
West Berlin 166-8; *see also* Berlin
White Russia 11, 12

Yalta conference 24
Yugoslavia, Federal People's Republic of (since 1963, Socialist Federal Republic), agriculture 31, 131, 134-5, establishments and first years 16, 18-22, 31, 35, economic development 89-90, 118, 126-8, 135, 147, economic problems 127, 132-3, 136-7, 150, League of Communists 126, 129, 137, living standards 138, 140-3, relation to socialist countries 35, 50, 52, 88, self-management model 100, 126-31; Kingdom of 20, 134, Communist Party of Yugoslavia 18, 40, economic development 14, 15, nationality problem 11, 12, political development 11, 13, World War Two 16, 31

Zagorje 126
Zog (King of Albania) 20
Zogu, Ahmed 13
Zyclon, B. 17